UNDER THE RED BLANKET

The Story of My Family's Life in Northeast India

Bea Anderson Swedien

First edition published in 2011

Paperback ISBN 978-178092-003-0

Mobipocket ISBN 978-1-78092-004-7

ePub ISBN 978-1-78092-005-4

Published in the UK by MX Publishing

335 Princess Park Manor, Royal Drive, London, N11 3GX

www.mxpublishing.com

ACKNOWLEDGEMENTS

My heartfelt thanks to my fun-loving parents, Bengt and Edna Anderson, who gave us a storybook childhood in the wilds of India and saved the memories in their diaries and letters.

Thanks also to my husband Bruce and daughter Roberta, who never complained on hearing the stories of my life in the jungle. Without their encouragement and help, this book would never have been written.

My sisters June and Audrey and brother Jim contributed their experiences with good humour and a shared love of India.

Adding their expertise to the project were Gareth Maynard, Bridget Morton, Bjorn Asplind, Trond Braaten and Laura Davis. The cover photo of the Naga shawl is by Mark Emery.

Dedicated to my brother Bruce, who was my best friend
and loved India dearly, but left us too soon.
I still miss him.

THE BUNGALOW AT IMPUR

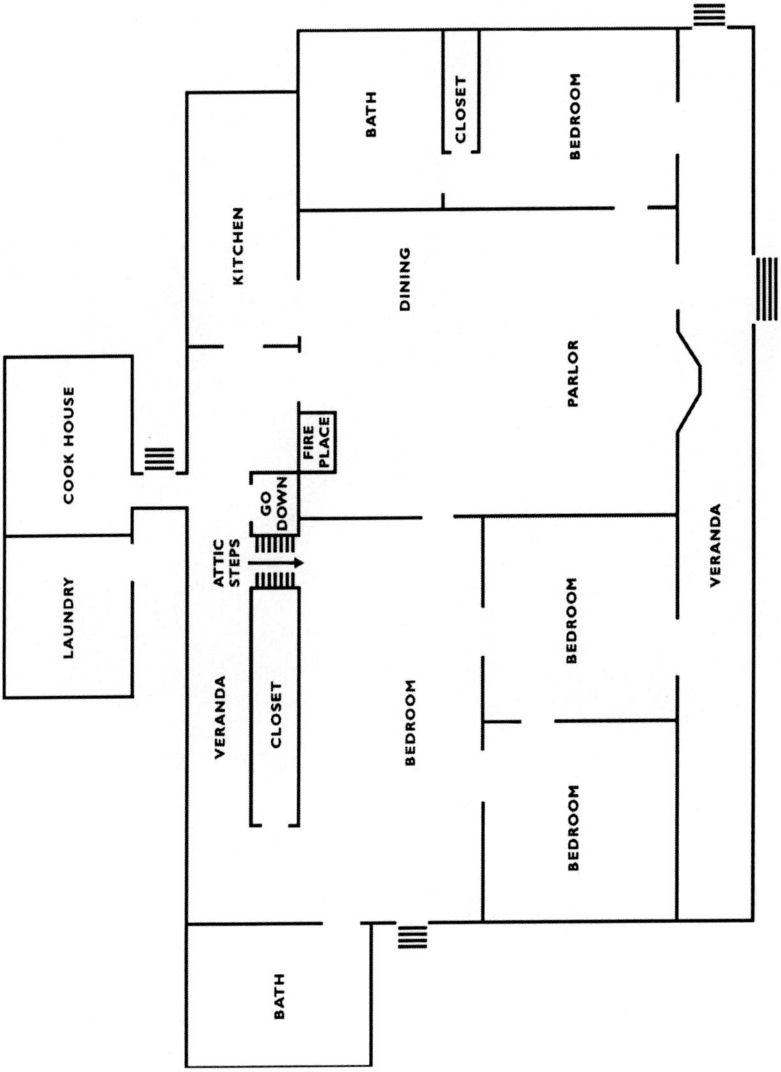

MAP OF ASSAM

Map of Assam before Nagaland was a State

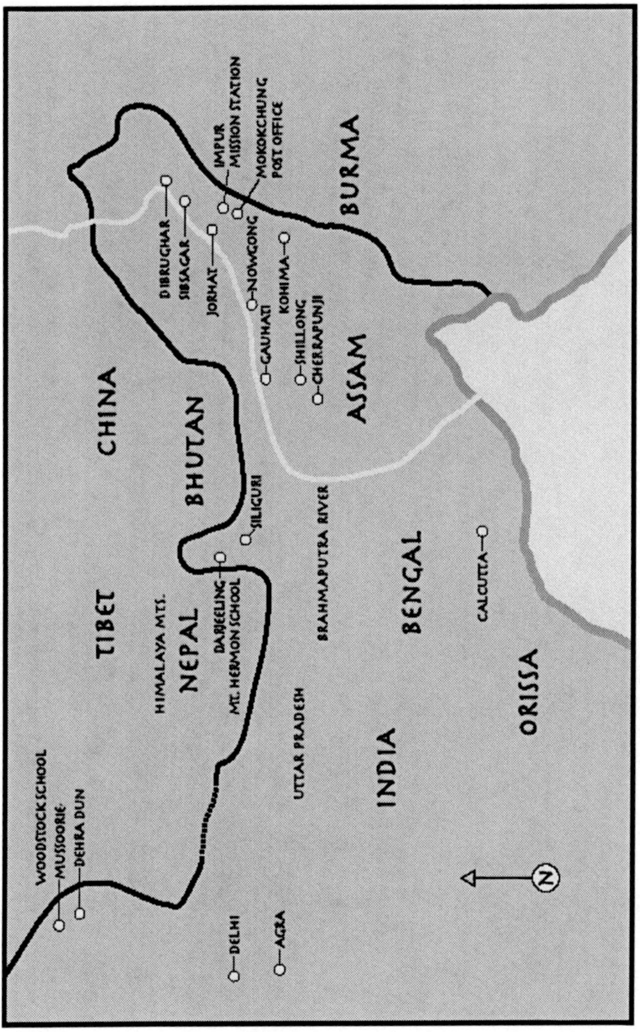

THE NAGA HILLS

A prose poem by Jim Anderson

In the lavender hush of the beginning of time, the young hills stood naked, disrobed and silent, for there was none to hear the great spirit say:

"I will cover these hills with garments of green and will fill the forests with living creatures, large and small and the valley's cleavage will resound to the moving of water under a canopy of wind swept clouds of monsoons. The very hilltops will be home to a thousand villages of warriors, who chant as they move into battle and the forests will echo with the songs of workers in the fields. It will take the strength of stone to survive and they will be strong. It will take boldness and bravery to succeed and they will be the bravest of all men.

"Fearing no one, they will forever put fear in the hearts of those who live in the Great Valley and can only speak of death to those who would venture into the hills. For here is the abode of a people apart, living to preserve their freedom and joy in the innocence of primitive splendor."

And in time did the lavender hush of the beginning become the brilliant gold of ten thousand suns shining on a thousand hilltops, garmented in green, divided by rivers of silver, whereon did live the chosen strong, brave and bold.

India: land of poverty and riches, an old land of contrasts and contradictions. Breathe deep of its animals, people; open eyes and minds to what is here and nowhere else. It's the same India before the Great War, before independence in the days of the Raj. How could so few govern so many in such diverse circumstances and still have opportunities to enjoy the rivers, mountains, plains, hills and jungles of maybe the most interesting country in the world? Northeast

India, specifically, where the mighty or muddy Brahmaputra River, after an uninspired beginning high in the Himalayas, finds its way between mountains on three sides to form the valley of Assam, buffered on its east by the Naga Hills. Only the sky above and the sea at the end of its journey, know its course. The rain on a canopy of green, thunder at eventide, or is it the throbbing cadence of drums? The blue hills in the chill of morn slowly change colour by the rosy spears of dawn, the mist silently rising to meet a warming sun.

These are the memories we easily keep and love. To own from the hidden dwelling place of my youth.

FOREWARD

By Roberta Swedien

My mother can catch a fly with her bare hands. Every time. A resounding, startling "Thwap!" and the buzzing stops. She can also speak Ao Naga, tell tales of headhunting tribes, man-eating tigers and journeys through the jungle. She rides bareback, hates wearing shoes, has a passion for animals and nature and an amazing appetite for life.

Like an alchemist, she can brew up curry, cloves and chicken into a feast worthy of the chiefs. Blonde and blue eyed, my mother is part Naga. She grew up in the Naga Hills of northeast India in the 1930s – 1950s. Lush mountain jungle inhabited by former headhunting tribes, this was a land of legend and mystery, wisdom and instinct, hard life and heroic adventure. Her childhood was extraordinary and, as a result, so was mine.

Massive old photograph albums in our American home had my young imagination spellbound for hours: sepia images of dark, fearless men clutching spears, women draped in beads, open-jawed leopards and wild boar displayed after the hunt, a sea of Nagas at a village gathering and in their midst, astoundingly, my very own family - my mother wearing blonde braids and a little girl's topee. Tucked away in our Chicago basement was my grandfather's battered leather suitcase. On special occasions it was opened and the old red Naga blankets were brought out for everyone to see and touch. I was convinced they had magical powers. Now and then we had visitors from this mysterious land of my mother's youth. Short, vigorous, almond-eyed men from the other side of the world would sit at our dinner table and share vivid stories of the past.

Like a quiet sponge, I drank it all in. I am so happy she

has decided to tell this story of those years in that strange and wonderful place. I travelled back with her recently. It was an unforgettable experience. In the town of Impur, home to the tribe of the Aos, she stood alone on a platform in front of thousands of Nagas and in their native tongue, with great flourish and gesture, shouted, "Welcome, Ao Nagas, to the celebration!" She was home.

India has been my home for more than a decade. I have Naga friends and my own suitcase full of red shawls. I have yet to master the art of fly removal... but what's that buzzing I hear?

"Thwap!"

Ah, life is good. I am forever grateful.

Roberta Swedien
Pune, India
June 2004

Contents

A tiger killed in our village

1
GO AND LOOK AT THE DEAD TIGERS

As a child, I had a terrible fear of tigers. At night I would lie in my bed, with the kerosene lamp turned low and if a gentle breeze moved the cotton curtains at the door, I would imagine a tiger walking in to eat me. I could hear the hooting of owls and the howling of jackals in the valley below the bungalow and closer, the quieter sounds of my family reading or playing games in the front room.

The threat of tigers was real enough. The village behind our compound in Assam in northeast India was called Mopungchukit and quite often the villagers would kill tigers that preyed on their cattle. Typically, the Nagas mounted a dead tiger on a bamboo frame, lashing the massive body with vines and opening the dead mouth in a threatening grimace, to warn other tigers away from the herd. Once, when I was five or six, the villagers killed five tigers, which they impaled on bamboo sticks on the outskirts of the village. My brothers and two sisters, all older, thought it a great lark to go and look at the dead tigers and they insisted I accompany them. Jongpong, our dhobi or laundryman, thinking he could overcome my terror, carried me piggyback - and screaming - up the hill to view the dead tigers. More years than I like to admit later, I tell people I think tigers are quite beautiful and in need of protection. However, no tigers, dead or alive, have visited me lately.

The people of the village were of the Ao Naga tribe, reputed to be savage headhunters by some, but known to me as friends.

The Nagas would eat just about any meat, except that of

the tiger. They believed that some tigers had a secret human 'partner', who might be living among them in the village. In Naga lore, if the tiger or the man died suddenly, his 'partner' would immediately die as well. The villagers seemed to know which tigers shared the soul of a neighbor and these tigers were rarely threatened.

There were plenty of tigers and leopards in the jungles adjacent to our house. The natives did not distinguish between the two species, calling the tiger "the big one" and the leopard "the little one". An experienced hunter would rather face a tiger than a leopard, because a cornered tiger will seek escape, whereas a leopard fights to the end. Even if a hunter survived a fight with a leopard, he faced the likelihood of deadly infection from wounds inflicted by the leopard's claws, which harbour bacteria from rotten meat. The Nagas respected the leopard's persistence and cunning, knowing that the 'little one' would watch and wait for an opportunity to attack again.

These people and their customs made up much of what I knew of life as a child. I did not speak English till I was five because Tsungkumla, my ayah, spoke to me in the Ao Naga language. It's one of twelve languages spoken by the people with whom my parents worked as Baptist missionaries in India from 1926 - 1954.

Most people think of India as a land teeming with humanity. Many picture holy men, temples and sacred cows. Most know the associations of snake charmers with a cobra in a basket and Maharajahs, with incredible wealth, riding elephants in procession. Some may even imagine fertile fields, fruitful valleys, whispering palm trees, deep jungles and ponds laden with lotus blossoms. But in the northeast lies a part of old India less well-known, where the landscape is dominated by the towering Himalayas. Here, in one of the most beautiful parts of India, is the state known as Nagaland, rarely visited by outsiders.

Many different tribes inhabit this section of northeastern India and they incorporate a wide range of religions, culture, languages and social systems. One of these cultures is a tribal group known as Nagas. For centuries, the Nagas were warring headhunting tribes. Animists, the Nagas traditionally worshipped nature and offered sacrifices to spirits, both good and evil.

No one really knows where the name ‘Naga’ comes from. One theory is that it is from the Burmese ‘Na-Ka’, meaning people with pierced earlobes - a widespread practice among all the Naga tribes. Another is that it comes from the Assamese word for naked – ‘noga’. A third theory, though less probable, is that the name came from the Sanskrit word ‘nag’, which means snake.

As for the people themselves, neither anthropologists nor British colonial officials have been able to clearly identify the roots of the Naga people. Who are these Nagas and from where do they come?

They have skin the colour of café au lait, with high cheekbones and Asian eyes. They build their villages on mountaintops so they can see any enemies before they arrive and they cultivate crops along the hillsides. They travel daily to rivers in the valley for water, which they carry up the mountain in hollowed-out bamboo, so all the people have strong legs, tight buttocks and great endurance. My ayah, whom I last saw in 1996, is still alive in her nineties. Some suspect these people came from Borneo, or even the Philippines, but how they might have arrived in northeast India, no one can say. The Nagas are not a single homogenous people, but a composite of some eighteen tribes speaking about thirty dialects and with different customs.

Their diet consists primarily of rice, pork, greens and eggs, although, at times, they also eat grubs and insects. They are, by and large, happy and carefree, with an extraordinary capacity for enjoying life. They laugh frequently and they love to sing, often chanting a call and response, "oh-he-ho", in musical thirds as they work. My father often speculated that they chanted to ward off marauding jungle animals.

Traditionally, the Nagas believe that some spirit inhabits all things, animate or inanimate, though the Sema tribe also believed in an unseen higher power. When my parents first came to India, before I was born, the natives told them about a rock in the area that was so powerful that, if anyone touched it, he or she would die. Intending to prove them wrong, a missionary defied their belief and kissed the rock. He died of typhoid within a year - a fact the Nagas impressed on my parents early.

The Nagas are a proud and strong-willed people. Each village has a chief who has absolute power over them, but the people often fought, even village to village. After the British came to India, Naga raiders would attack British tea gardens on the plains. By the mid-1800s, the British government, in an effort to control the headhunters, undertook a few military operations into the hills, but these tactics often failed. After that, the British began to restrict entry to the Naga Hills.

They also refused to allow the tribal people to come down from the mountains to the plains to barter for salt, kerosene and occasionally steel for spears. Some even say that the British secretly hoped the mountain tribes would kill each other off.

Certainly, the British neither understood nor accepted the Naga belief that by killing a man and taking his head, one gained the dead man's power.

An Ao Naga chief wearing an elephant tusk armband, a cowrie shell wristband and a wild gardenia in his ear.

Human skulls adorning a chief's house

Human and methan [wild buffalo] skulls on a morung post

Inaho, a Sema with an Angami teacher

"Under the Red Blanket" - my father with a delegation of chiefs

Eventually, as the British realised the value of negotiating only with the headman in each village, they took to giving each chief a red wool blanket to wear, making him easy to identify. These blankets became a symbol of authority and pride to the Naga people. Thus, when my family arrived in India, we first came to know the people living *under the red blanket.*

Headhunting was still practiced by several Naga tribes at least until 1958 and has occurred in many cultures. The Nagas regarded the man who took the most heads as their greatest warrior. When one considers that by taking a head, one captures the other man's strength, the custom seems, if not more palatable, at least more understandable. Sometimes the Nagas also enslaved or sacrificed their prisoners. All these practices earned them both curiosity and reprobation from the world beyond the hills. Less well-known was the fact that these people have a deep faith that the soul transmigrates after the death of each person and the head is the receptacle of the soul. The Nagas honour the head as an object of immense vitality and a source of creative energy. When the Nagas brought the heads of their slain enemies home, they poked a hole in each skull to release evil spirits. The cleaned skulls were then mounted on the front of each warrior's house as a symbol of his courage and strength. In the villages near our bungalow, some warriors had as many as forty heads mounted on the front of their thatched houses. Terrifying as these grisly ornaments were, we soon learned it was necessary to understand the people's customs so we could relate to them and they to us. Several of the best and most faithful warriors on our hill station and in the surrounding villages were reformed headhunters.

Among these was Inaho, a famous Sema chief. I remember being entertained by him during a Mungdong, or tribal convention. This was when the Nagas gathered en masse in a basha, or temporary shelter, which was open on all sides, constructed of bamboo and thatched over with palm fronds. Sometimes as many as 1,500 Nagas from many tribes would gather under a basha to discuss joint issues and mission concerns. My father used these gatherings as an opportunity to preach. Sometimes this required as many as four interpreters, simultaneously translating for the several tribes. All this seemed extremely boring to me as a child. Inaho, seeing that I was restless, would take palm fronds left over from the construction of the basha and whittle small animals for me to play with in the dust. However fierce he may have been as a headhunter,

Inaho was attentive and generous to the tiny blonde daughter of the people who had converted him, or nearly so. Later, my parents were both understandably upset when Inaho, one of their most dedicated disciples, took a second wife - a practice not uncommon among the Semas.

Since the British did not spend as much time among the Nagas and with bigamy common and headhunting rampant, the colonial authorities were not always willing or able to patrol the Naga Hills. However, when tea plantations encroached on the hills, the British government once again was forced to connect with the Naga natives. A border was maintained beyond which the Nagas were allowed to headhunt without retaliation, but our safety could not be guaranteed should we go beyond these borders. In any case, travel through the dense jungles was always difficult, so little was known beyond the hills of these primitive tribes. But with the outbreak of World War II, the American military established an air base in Jorhat, three days' journey from our village by horseback and the Nagas became valuable as guides for military operations and, eventually, air rescue. Many a downed flyer owed his life to the skill of these tribesmen, as journalist Eric Sevareid reported in 'Not So Wild A Dream'. This book details his adventures when he and others bailed out of a military plane bound for China and lived for a month "with savage headhunters." These so-called 'savages' included my ayah and my playmates, who, after partial subjugation, were subjects of the King, until 1947, when they came under the rule of newly independent India.

After the British left, in the early days of Indian independence, the Nagas expressed a desire for their own independence, but the new government of India refused to consider it. A prolonged and bloody conflict ensued in the 1950s. This conflict ultimately led to my parents being forced out of India.

In 1963, their beloved territory became Nagaland, a new state of India, but the fight for Naga independence continues even today, with skirmishes between Indian soldiers and Naga rebels. This book is the story of our lives among the Nagas, whom I still consider to be my family and their hills to be my home.

My great-grandparents Anderson in Sweden

Lunch in the Swedish woods

2
BENGT AND EDNA PREPARE

My father, Bengt Anderson, was born in 1896 in his grandparents' little red farmhouse in Högstad town, Östergotland, Sweden. There was little celebration about his birth, as he was the illegitimate child of a teenage daughter and his grandparents, Johan and Christina, had already raised three sons and four daughters. Young Bengt's father left for Stockholm before my father was born, ostensibly to find work. Dad did not meet his own father until he was fifty-four. I witnessed this encounter when we returned to Sweden in 1950 at the beginning of our furlough to the States. One day, a school friend of my father's unexpectedly approached him, saying an old man had been asking questions about him and his visiting family. The friend offered to give Dad an address. Soon Dad, Mother, my brother and I travelled to a small red house in the middle of a Swedish forest, where my father met his father, Alben Bloom, for the first time.

How strange it seemed then, as now, that my father could have spent an entire lifetime without the love and care of his parents. Even at sixteen, I depended on the warmth of my father's humour and his sustaining kindness. I remember the way my grandfather's eyes filled with tears, as he recalled his love for Amanda, my father's mother, whom he had abandoned before my father was born. We later calculated that my grandfather had fathered at least seven children among three women, though he only married once, so far as we know.

Young Bengt Anderson grew up bearing his mother's maiden name, toddling behind his grandmother and helping his grandfather around the farm. He often recalled climbing a large hill, known as Klemmingsberget, behind the farmhouse. From the top of this hill, he would watch farmers in the fields or on their way to market, all the while wondering what lay off in the distance. I sometimes think his early ventures up that hill must have influenced his later love for the mountains of India. I feel sure his grandparents must have loved him, since he showed no signs of abandonment or loss as long as I knew him.

My father did well in school as a boy. This was helpful, since his grandparents knew only what they had taught themselves. Soon he was given the task of reading and writing letters for them - a frequent task, since six of their children had emigrated to the United States. My father loved to read the letters they sent home, as he was isolated and lonely on the farm. His own mother had remained in Sweden, but she left him with his grandparents and never revealed who his father was. His mother only returned for him after she married a Baptist preacher, when she wanted to use him for labour. Though our father never mentioned this, before her death, his cousin Maja told us that, at the age of twelve, my father attended school during the day and worked most of the night in his mother's basement, printing literature for the Baptist church. His mother insisted on this until a neighbour reported it to the authorities. After that, Bengt was sent back to his grandparents' hardscrabble farm, where, at times, his grandmother, lacking flour, ground birch bark for bread. My father's malnutrition was so severe that, though he was tall at 6'2", he had the birdcage chest typical of rickets.

Young Bengt rarely saw his mother, who died of tuberculosis when he was a teenager. Despite these and other hardships, my father never complained about anything in his entire life, except the Indian babus, or merchants. "Confound it," he would yell in frustration, when, as always, the babus drove a hard bargain for the tin we needed for the roof or other supplies essential to our mission compound.

My father was eager to continue his education, but he knew there was little chance of that in Sweden. He was delighted when his Aunt Hedda, who worked as a cook for the Roosevelt family in Hyde Park, New York, visited Sweden in 1915. Later on, Hedda and her husband invested in the stock market and became quite wealthy, though when the market crashed in 1929, Hedda went into her kitchen and killed herself by turning on the gas. But in 1915, she encouraged my father to leave Sweden, which he did that year, travelling with her.

Afterwards, my father wrote poignantly of his regret at leaving the farm, where the old rooster crowed and skylarks sang above the stubborn oxen plowing the fields. He would always miss the runestones that stand in fields all over Sweden - those large slabs of granite carved by Vikings more than a thousand years before his birth, some with the sign of the cross. Even as a young man, my father's faith seems to have been strong. I have often wondered if that faith developed in response to his loneliness as a child. Anyway, he told me often that memories of his childhood home were a big help when he faced new and deeper loneliness in the new world.

Before this trip, my father had only travelled on foot or by bicycle on country lanes near his home. But in September 1915, he travelled by train to Bergen, Norway, where he boarded the SS Kristianiafjord, bound for

America. This may have been the first time that Dad's strange magnetic pull for adventure revealed itself, because some distance into the North Sea, his ship was stopped by a British cruiser. The officers ordered the ship to change course to the Orkney Islands. World War I was raging in Europe and even ships from neutral countries could not travel freely. All the passengers were interrogated and some were ordered off the ship. Mail was confiscated, but finally the Kristianiafjord was allowed to weigh anchor and return to sea.

When at last they entered New York harbour, my father, with the other passengers, excitedly watched the ship sail past the Statue of Liberty, her torch held high. His eyes filled with tears at her generous welcome to strangers from foreign shores. He used to tell us his Aunt Hedda smiled at his enthusiasm, but she also warned that he'd need to work hard to find his fortune, even in America. Luckily, my father never shrunk from hard work, nor did his enthusiasm for Sweden and his adopted countries, both India and the United States, ever waver.

Dad entered through Ellis Island, but he left the New York area quickly, afraid he might somehow be shipped back to Sweden. He went to Warren, PA, to live with relatives. He became active in a Swedish Baptist Church there and found work in a furniture factory. Soon a friend from church recommended him for a job with a wealthy lawyer, H.W. Allen, who hired Dad as a chauffeur. Besides driving and maintaining a Buick Roadster and Pierce-Arrow limousine, my father's other duties included caring for a cow and the garden. He often chatted with the Allen's young daughter as he worked and he learned rudimentary English from her.

Knowing of my father's interest in missionary work, his pastor in Pennsylvania suggested he apply to Bethel Academy, a private high school and seminary in Saint Paul, Minnesota, supported by the Swedish Baptist Church. Encouraged by Bethel, my father managed to earn his train fare to Saint Paul. There, in the two brick buildings that comprised Bethel, he studied English grammar and reading, along with Greek and Bible studies. Meanwhile, he also worked to help pay his tuition and board. He felt lucky to have a job waiting tables at the seminary, instead of having to work off-campus. Years later, Mother would plead, "Bengt, please take a rest." "Jag skall sova i graven", he always teased her in Swedish - "I shall sleep in the grave."

My parents' wedding

After his graduation from Bethel Academy in 1921, Dad travelled to the small town of Alexandria, Minnesota, to work as an assistant pastor in the church. While there, he stayed in a hotel run by Lars and Marie Michaelson, Swedish immigrants like himself, whose many children worked in the hotel and restaurant. Dad's attention was soon drawn to the Michaelson's second daughter, vivacious, red-haired Edna. He used to say that when he asked my mother to marry him, she replied that she was too busy to say anything but "yes." My mother, always forthright, called my father "a handsome Swede". Handsome he was: tall and lean, with wide blue eyes and a finely chiselled face. They agreed to marry as soon as they could and enter mission work together. My mother decided to enter nursing school in Saint Paul for a three-year course, knowing that nursing would serve them in their work.

Several years after they met, when my father had earned his high school diploma and had graduated from the seminary, my parents were able to marry. During their first years of marriage, Dad served as pastor in Kulm, North Dakota and my mother offered her services to the people as a nurse. Their first child, a daughter, was stillborn and buried there. They hoped at first to serve in missions in Russia, but that dream never materialised. When the pioneer missionary, Dr O.L. Swanson, spoke at their church, they learned of the American Baptists' foreign mission in Assam, India.

In 1926, they applied and were accepted for this mission, just before the birth of my sister, June. They spent that summer adjusting to life with their new baby and preparing for their life's dream - their long-awaited journey to India.

3
PASSAGE TO INDIA

In her diary, my mother described their departure from Minnesota: "I shall never forget the scene; my mother holding our little baby June, who was only six weeks old and my father's familiar features blurred by my tears. My brothers and sisters were weeping and waving as the train pulled away from the depot." She wrote of the train: the "journey was long and tiring, the baby was restless, my heart was sad and both of us cried at times." She told of a kind woman who helped her put June to sleep, "an art", she admitted she had, "not mastered as yet, but would soon have to learn." I have a hard time envisioning my mother so unsure of herself, as my experience of her was that she met every situation with resolve. Not only that, being of good Swedish stock, she had a quick and bawdy sense of humour whenever faced with difficulty, though she might weep at the sound of an Irish ballad. At 'O Danny Boy' in particular, she would laugh and weep all at once.

One can only imagine the trials my mother faced travelling by train across the United States with a baby in 1926, but those inconveniences paled in comparison to her first voyage to India. In New York on 7th September 1926, my parents and six-week-old June boarded the ship, 'City of Harvard', which Mother, in classic understatement, said, "was not the flagship of the Atlantic fleet". Ever honest, she did praise the stewards for their friendly efficiency. My parents soon learned that most of the passengers aboard the ship were missionaries and their faith was soon tested when cotton bales in the cargo hold ignited from the tremendous heat below decks. Lifeboats were kept in readiness and drills were ordered daily, though the captain assured the anxious passengers he would keep the blaze under control. Each day, his faithful passengers gathered to pray and after many sleepless nights and restless days, the ship pulled into Gibraltar, where the smouldering cargo was unloaded. Not until the ship passed the famous fortress and dropped anchor in the harbour's calm waters did the missionaries give up their vigil.

Mother on board the "City of Harvard", 1926

My mother recorded in her journal that my father purchased a beautiful piece of silk while they were ashore, which she made into a dress. It touches me that such a simple purchase could mean so much to her. She also noted that the mothers had little chance to notice geography as the ship sailed through the Mediterranean. On board, there was no laundry room, so she, like the other women, washed nappies in their cabins and hung the "white flags," as they called them, on deck to dry.

She used to tell us that in Port Said, Egypt, the fun began. Hoards of traders came in small boats to tempt them with trinkets and when the passengers were at last allowed ashore, they were quickly surrounded by guides and galli boys, or magicians, who, she told us, might have been descendants of Moses. She quickly realised their chief objective seemed to be to relieve gullible travellers of cash, so they couldn't have had much interest in all these missionaries, whose resources were scarce. I know from my own subsequent travels that the vocal game of salesmanship is eternal and universal, just as Mother described it, so many years ago.

The ship's first stop in India was Karachi (now in Pakistan), which seemed to my parents even stranger than the Middle East. After that, they sailed to Bombay, the main port of entry for most foreigners coming to India by ship at that time. From there, they boarded a train for Calcutta, but not before facing the first onslaught of beggars and coolies seeking baksheesh. My mother's sympathy, as she recorded in her journal, "was not with the beggars as much as with the coolie women who carried coal to the ships in the harbour. Old women, young women with babies, all loaded with heavy baskets of coal on their heads, walking up steep ladders, while the men stood idle or heaped abuse on the poor victims of India's strange culture." This observation demonstrates not only my mother's early and keen perception of how cultures must differ, but also her sense of herself already as a strong woman. This flexibility and strength, so typical of Mother, helped her children develop independence and strength as well.

This first journey to Calcutta introduced my parents to train travel in India - no small undertaking even now. In 1926, it required carrying one's own bedding, mosquito nets, drinking water and food, but offered no protection from bedbugs or cockroaches. Meals were served in the dining car, but there was no passage between cars. My parents could not leave their luggage unguarded in their compartment and the dining car could only be reached from the platform when the train stopped, so they were forced to take turns eating. At stations, the designated diner had to push a pathway through the crowds teeming on the platform, hoping to locate the dining car and sit down to eat in elegant British fashion, before rushing back through the crowd and somehow finding the right compartment before the train left the station. Often, this left at least one of them hungry and remember, my mother was nursing her baby. The trains had limited water for washing bodies or nappies, because dust from the track and soot from the steam engines rendered most sanitation impossible, however greatly desired. To use the toilet, one squatted over a hole in the floor of the train compartment - a custom unchanged when I revisited India as recently as 1996. How Victorian Englishwomen managed such travel is a predicament I can only imagine. No wonder they wore so many skirts!

Among my parents' travelling companions were their fellow missionaries and friends, Ruth and August Berg and their baby, all of whom had sailed to India with them. When this large group arrived, tired and hungry at Howrah station in Calcutta, they arranged for taxis to take them to the Lee Memorial Mission, where they arrived quite late at night. Though they longed desperately for a hot meal, they were told they would not be served breakfast until six in the morning, in their rooms. Typically, my parents always said they were happy that at least June and the other nursing baby, Roger Berg, could eat.

Mrs Lee, a "motherly" woman, according to my own efficient mother, ran a school for girls and an inn for itinerant missionaries in Calcutta. She dedicated the school to her six children, who, while attending boarding school in Darjeeling, had died in a landslide. One child survived long enough to describe their terror as the children and their ayah held hands in their cottage, awaiting certain death. One girl could only be identified by her small hand, with its recognisable ring. The child who survived longest died of tetanus; at the end he could only take water by sucking on a sponge. In the family room of the school hung two large pictures of these children. My mother, so far from home and a new parent herself, spent hours contemplating those young faces, worried not only about June's safety, but also the lives of the other children my parents hoped to have.

In Calcutta, my parents bade farewell to the Bergs, who were sent to a different part of India. They also went to purchase supplies at New Market, a very large open-air market with many stalls selling all sorts of food and household goodies. This terrified my mother enough for her to mention it in her journal: "crowds everywhere, cows roaming the streets, beggars and dogs on the sidewalks and noise, what a commotion! The filthy eating places with swarms of flies and hornets, the aroma of mustard oil and other spices, the constant blaring of taxi horns and the call of coolies and store keepers, trying to entice us into their shops." She reported all this made her dizzy. Characteristically, she also ended, "It was fun."

A typical Naga village

A 1993 re-enactment: tribal dancers are wearing headdresses of bearskin adorned with hornbill feathers, sashes of goat hair dyed red and loin cloths covered in cowrie shells

The next part of their trip, by rickety train from Calcutta, took them through Siliguri and on to Amingaon, a ferry point on the bank of the Brahmaputra River, where they had to climb down from the train and clamber through loose sand to the ferry, trusting the coolies to follow with their belongings. What amazement! Once on board and on the upper deck, they found an elegant dining room where turbaned and white-coated bearers served a delicious fresh fish dinner in the most elegant British style, with linen-covered tables and sterling silver cutlery. I still have bone handled and engraved fish knives and servers, which I first learned to use on that ferry, in one of the remotest parts of India.

On the other side of the river, my parents at long last were met by Mr Olney, treasurer of the Baptist Mission in

Assam, which would be their home and eventually mine.

By the time the family reached Assam, my father had contracted dysentery. As a nurse, my mother trusted he would recover fairly quickly, but she knew the nausea from which she suffered might last longer, as she was once again pregnant. She wrote in her journal that she had no appetite, though she ought to have been eating for two. The next year my brother, Jim, would be born in Jorhat. Besides her third pregnancy, my mother was also dealing with diabetes, as she had her entire life.

Throughout her travels, then and later, Mother gave herself insulin shots daily. Somehow she always managed her restricted diet and varying cultures without comment. Around this time, while in Gauhati - a mission station where my parents awaited assignment - she also discovered an odd inability to perspire. This condition eventually required my parents' placement in the Naga Hills, I know I should not rejoice in anyone's misfortune, particularly my own mother's. Still, I'd choose the Naga Hills over perspiration any day.

In Gauhati, she and my father studied the Assamese language, which they soon realised would not come easily. I try to imagine the frustrations of this young couple, unfamiliar with the country, the people, the climate and even mission policies. They must have felt such relief when they were finally sent to Jorhat, in the foothills of Naga country. In her journal, Mother described her first impression of the tea gardens there, "where rows of tea bushes miles in length extended in all directions." In the shade of the groves, they "saw the large bungalow and sheds of the garden centers... In between the bushes were scores of women plucking leaves, dressed in colorful saris and carrying large baskets of tea leaves on their heads." Towards the horizon and close to their long journey's end, they saw for the first time the luxuriant Naga Hills.

Within a couple of stations, they also encountered strangers, nearly naked, with features unlike any Indians they had yet seen. My parents were immediately fascinated by these people. The men wore scanty dress, at least by these outsiders' standards. They looked almost naked, with little more than a G-string across their loins. Mother wrote at the time that this did not appeal to her sense of modesty, not that I ever noticed she had one. The men carried huge bamboo spears with metal tips and powerful machetes my parents soon learned were called daos. On their arms they wore ivory armlets, crosscut from elephant tusks and in their ears, they wore ornaments of brass. Their hair was worn short, almost in a bowl cut, sometimes a bit longer at the front or back of the head. Some even had frightening tattoos across their cheeks or foreheads. Only later did my parents discover that a warrior could only earn a tattoo by taking the head of an enemy.

Ever alert to cultural distinctions, Mother quickly noticed that the women carried all the heavy loads in big cone-shaped baskets, which they attached to a headband, so their backs supported all the weight. Mother was immediately curious about their customs, wanting to know what their villages and the homes they lived in looked like. Both parents wondered how successful they would be as missionaries. They already knew that others had preceded them. The first, Dr E.W. Clarke, arrived in 1878, with no support from any congregations at home, to minister to these reclusive mountain tribes. First, Dr Clarke started a school in a large headhunter village. Early in his time with the Nagas, Dr Clarke worried nightly that he might be taken as a slave or worse, since he learned the tribal customs soon enough. Yet his courage impressed the Nagas, many of whom watched him with respect bordering on awe. These proud people did not take to the missionary's moral teachings quickly, though.

After a while, Dr Clarke asked some elders if he and a few of his converts could build their own small village some distance away in the jungle. He hoped that there, other believers or interested people might visit him. The local chief gave permission, but he did not hesitate to point out that this new village would not have any protection. Dr Clarke and his faithful followers risked being burned out or murdered by marauding tribes as they cleared some land and built their own new village. People from the other villages saw with surprise that the Christians' crops grew high in the fields without benefit of human sacrifice. They also saw how peacefully the new villagers lived together and how little they seemed to fear attack by other Nagas. Dr Clarke helped cure disease and this endeared him to the Nagas as well, particularly to the Ao and Angami tribes, who began to listen carefully to his Christian readings. Dr Clarke hoped first to eliminate headhunting, slavery and the rice beer that encouraged so much aggression. He worried less about nudity and other customs that one might think would have horrified a Victorian Christian.

Despite Dr Clarke's and my parents' efforts, no missionaries reside today in this part of Assam. All responsibility for the education and culture of the people has returned to its rightful place in the hands of the Naga nationals. These stalwart people have shown great courage in times of tremendous hardships, as they struggle to maintain tribal ways while the world changes around them. I saw this when I returned for the centennial celebration they held for Dr Clarke's work.

4
THE COMPOUND AT NORTH LAKHIMPUR

By 1927, my parents had received their first assignment in North Lakhimpur. They travelled there by Model T Ford, because Mr Firth, to whom the car was assigned and who lived where they were headed, preferred to travel by oxcart. Among the many rivers on this journey was the Subansiri, which they crossed aboard a ferry so flimsy it seemed likely to sink with them and all their belongings. Naturally, the current intensified as they approached the Himalayas and the river carried many trees along with it. Once the people and their gear were aboard the ferry, workers pulled the makeshift craft along the shore for about half a mile and then set out across the rapids. The ferry picked up speed in the current and seemed likely to sink. My mother was terrified, but an accident on board distracted her. She watched a man anoint, Hindu fashion, a deep gash in his leg with fresh cow dung. Bursting into action, Mother ran to him and removed the dung, so she could pour a liberal dose of iodine from her medical kit over the wound. Then she applied a fresh, clean bandage to the man's leg. By the time she finished attending to the man's wound, the ferry had landed with a jolt and they looked forward to travelling overland, perhaps even without incident.

No such luck. As they drove away, a woman ran directly in front of the Model T and my father, unable to stop, drove right over her. Nearly hysterical, they stopped and rushed behind the car. Carefully, they lifted the frail woman, who seemed to be spitting blood, into the back seat. My mother ministered to the poor woman as best she could, while my father drove to the compound, where their new friend Mr Firth, greeted them with mystifying laughter. The woman, they soon learned, had rolled safely between the wheels of the car; the red liquid was paan, a paste of betel nut, lime and a certain leaf Indians commonly chew, supposedly to aid digestion. This refreshing concoction turns saliva red. Luckily, the woman was unharmed, or my parents' missionary career might have been over before it even started.

In the compound, they were expected to live with Mr Firth in his bungalow. When they arrived, as my father would recall, dust seemed to have settled over everything. The main room had a wooden-planked floor with wide cracks and small windows, with only a cloth nailed to the rafters as the ceiling. The room held a table, some chairs and an almirah, or cupboard, in which were stored a few dishes. At one end of the room stood a rusty old kerosene tin for bathing. A few inches of water were standing in it. Mr Firth's bedroom and office were on the other side of the house, which also had a spacious verandah in back. Interestingly, my mother was more struck by the bedroom, which had once been occupied by the Firths. Though Mrs Firth had been dead for some time, neither her clothes nor the bed had been touched, as Mr Firth could not face the task and the servants had conveniently overlooked it. Mother described Mr Firth in her journal as, "a gaunt and lonely old man, his sparse white beard and his features shaded by a large pith topee which he wore at all times." She thought he looked sad and lonely and she was determined to be his friend.

That night as they slept, Mother heard a noise in the thatch overhead. Though frightened of rats, she did not wake my father, who slept on. In the morning she asked Mr Firth about the rats. He assured her there could not be rats in the ceiling. When she wondered how that could be, he offered scant comfort: "The snakes in the thatch will eat any rats."

Mother with a servant and baby June with her ayah

Mother refused even to try to sleep the next night until my father investigated the noises overhead. The racket turned out to be a nest of young owls, squawking as their parents fed them. Mother's relief about the snakes didn't last long, however, because soon after, a young boy killed a large cobra near the bungalow. Later on, a snake charmer happened by. My mother's scream distracted the charmer, whose snake slithered under the verandah. It was reclaimed by the owner with some difficulty, but not soon enough to please her, as she continued to remind us throughout her years in India. Mother never acquired any emotional attachment to snakes, rats, or spiders.

In the compound, my parents learned more Assamese and began to adjust to the culture. They learned the compound was locked at night to protect the humans and animals within from jackals and even the occasional tiger on the prowl. Forever after, my mother hated jackals, which at night would approach the bungalows quietly and then give out a bloodcurdling howl that frightened both her and baby June. So, Mother remained close to the compound, while my father began preaching in nearby bazaars.

This was also their first encounter with British tea planters, who, for the most part, seemed to think the missionaries should not interfere with the natives. Dad used to say they worried they'd have no one to pick tea if the people were educated. After their long journey, my parents also delighted in their first letters from the States. In those days before transoceanic flights or phones, surface mail took at least four weeks to cross the ocean.

While in North Lakhimpur, my parents hired an ayah for June and they took the baby on at least one memorable outing. They went out to help Mr Firth, whom by now they called Uncle John. They stopped alongside a rice paddy when they saw his tent on the outskirts of a village. Some men rushed over to carry Mother across the paddy and my father waded barefoot through the flooded field, while the ayah was given strict instructions how to carry June across. Unfortunately, the woman slipped suddenly and fell. She dropped little June into the stagnant water, which was smelly and green with scum. The men held Mother back while one of them rescued the baby and quickly brought her to our mother, who hurried to Mr Firth's tent to change and comfort not only the baby, but very likely herself as well.

North Lakhimpur offered my parents their first opportunity to meet the Assamese people. My mother visited the town women of higher caste; lower caste women worked as coolies and tea pickers, so she was unable to meet so many of these women in the villages. My father could not visit the higher caste women in their homes because they were in purdah and could not be seen by any man who was not a member of the family.

Mother's new friends asked many questions and she tried to answer honestly, though she worried about the influence of the men, who came and went freely, with servants carrying any load, even items as light as a cane. My father used to laugh at the memory of one man whose servant carried his false teeth to a tea party.

By now, my family was facing their first Christmas in India and Mother feared it would be nothing like the celebrations in Minnesota she loved. They visited their friends, the Ahlquists, on Christmas Eve and found their bungalow decorated not only with wreaths and candles, but a decorated mahoe tree, with slender leaves like pine needles. The next day they were invited to a native feast of curry and rice, a meal served charmingly on banana leaves.

The lush, green Naga Hills

Unfortunately, Mother also developed a severe case of malaria in North Lakhimpur, which made her delirious. She was so seriously ill that Dad sent a telegram to the doctor in Jorhat, but the wires were down and a runner took three days to deliver the message. The doctors could only recommend large doses of quinine, which Mother was afraid to take because she was pregnant. Dad said she had visions of dying then, though she seemed surprised when the doctor told her later she might not have survived. She feared her health would never be strong enough for the isolation she might face in their final placement. Indeed, the doctors recommended that my parents return to Jorhat for Mother's health.

So, after a year in Mr. Firth's bungalow, they returned to Jorhat, sadly leaving behind their many dear friends in the compound.

Mother recovered nicely and my brother Jim was born in Jorhat on 29th February 1928, an eleven-pound leap year baby who managed to march to his own drummer from the start. He continues to entertain us to this day. Dad left my mother and both children in Jorhat while he returned to North Lakhimpur, where he again developed dysentery. This time it was bad enough for Mr Firth to send for the doctor, who insisted Dad be transported back to Jorhat, where he also developed a severe case of typhoid, which took several weeks to recover from.

Later that year, after his recovery, the Mission Board decided to send the family to the Naga Hills, where the Sema Naga tribe had recently given evidence of moving closer to Christianity. They would replace Dr Bailey there. He was the missionary who had died of typhoid after kissing the rock the Nagas said housed an evil spirit. Their territory in the hills would include several stations and encompass many tribes, living in more than a hundred villages and speaking many different languages. Their first station was in Kohima. Eventually, we would also live in Impur and Aizuto, all in the lush and mountainous region of the Naga Hills, rich in timber and other natural resources, including lime, coal and oil. Despite India's advanced civilisation, the Naga Hills lay uncharted and untouched by outside influences for centuries. The mountains there rise several thousand feet above sea level and the fresh mountain air remains cool throughout the year. Only in the 1930s did the land and its people really open up to exploration.

Of course, my parents entered their new assignment with their typical enthusiasm and fear. Dad, who never seemed to think about fear, would be forced to travel this huge territory on foot, leaving Mother alone with a few servants for weeks at a time, while he visited as many as ten to twelve tribes in the many villages hidden throughout the hills. Mother worried, quite naturally, that Dad might die far away from all of us. People had warned them about headhunters, but my mother, nurse that she was, worried much more about malaria and intestinal disorders. Beyond that, they both realised that Mother would never be described as robust. She had two young children and required several shots daily for the diabetes she had dealt with since childhood. And in that wild and dangerous territory, without benefit of electricity, running water, or any of the amenities most Westerners consider necessary, these two young people took on the added difficulty of learning several new languages, some barely catalogued.

5
HOME IN THE HILLS

Along the trail into the hills, the family stayed in what the people called dak bungalows. These dak bungalows were quaint two-room houses, built in villages for the use of government officials and maintained by a chowkidar [caretaker]. These houses were originally intended for British officers on patrol, but, if not occupied, were available for our use. Usually they held a steel bed or two without bedding, a few dishes, a table and a few chairs and a galvanised tub for bathing. A short distance away was a cookhouse with a chulha, or primitive grill for cooking. Nearby there was also a latrine, which my mother visited as little as possible, because while there she frequently encountered hundreds of spiders. A wooden box mounted on the wall of the dak bungalow held a guest book and occasionally, magazines left by British officers. One of the entries in the guest book, written by one of the visiting Brits was, "The latrine is too far from the bungalow." The next entry read, "You should have left sooner!" I have a low-slung teak chair on my patio because it reminds me of the chairs that sat on the veranda of dak bungalows.

The trip up to Kohima was also difficult because this was the first time my parents experienced traveling in double stages. In the village of Kolo, they found the native coolies waiting and complaining about the delay. Though my parents had planned to stop there for the night, the coolies gathered up their belongings and took off double-time, heading for the next village up the hill. My parents had no choice but to follow, though my mother was easily fatigued, as she was now pregnant again.

They were also amazed to discover that the Naga people eat no bread. Stopping along the trail, Dad cleaned a kerosene tin and Mother found some flour. Then he dug a hole in the ground and built a roaring fire, while Mother prepared the dough. In went the buns, for better or worse. He heaped the hot live coals over the tin and baked the bread and in due time they had fresh buns, vitamin enriched, frosted with ashes and spiced with kerosene. Quoting her father, who told her, "hunger was the best appetiser", Mother always claimed that those buns were the best she ever ate.

Toward the end of the trip, they met a man of the Rengma tribe carrying a loaded gun. He had been sent to protect them, as a man-eating tiger was on the prowl. Not all tigers prey on humans; usually only an old or injured animal will attack. My mother tartly asked if, "man-eating tigers also ate women?" She never told us the man's reply, only that they never saw that tiger. Lucky for them!

They visited many villages along their way, among them a Sema Naga village they could not enter because no Christians lived there. They camped along the roadside and the people came to them in search of medical care. They were able to offer quinine for malaria, iodine for wounds, drops for inflamed eyes and drugs to kill the intestinal worms endemic among the Nagas. They also carried painkillers for those whose ills they could not diagnose. One day, they encountered a large delegation of Nagas led by a chief in full native dress: a larger loincloth than usual (could it be that he was bragging?) with a sash made of goat hair, which had been dyed red, across his chest. He wore heavy ivory armbands and a necklace of wild boar tusks. In the chief's ears were brass rings. His headdress was of black bearskin, with black and white hornbill feathers attached to it. Despite his savage appearance, this man invited my father to come to his village and preach, offering hope for their missionary work.

A call to raid

The gaonbura, or village chief, told my father of an attack on his village by headhunters. Such attacks occurred frequently during gennas - festivals in the Sema tribe's calendar during which the people abstained from work and food to placate offended spirits. Gennas marked annual events like planting and harvests, as well individual events like childbirth or death. The chief explained that his village, Molung, clung to the east side of a range of steep mountains, forming the boundary between the Naga territory and the Ahom kingdom, later known as Assam.

While the people were sleeping, cattle dozed in the narrow street, contentedly chewing their cud; even the pigs and dogs had ceased fighting. All was peaceful. The light of the full moon transformed the rugged mountains into an enchanted land. Only the murmur of a distant stream and the eager call of a barking deer searching for a mate broke the silence. At Molung's locked gate squatted the village sentries, tending their fire by turns, confident because the young men had stacked their spears to rest undisturbed in their morung, or barracks, unaware that in the village of Tamlu, located on the next ridge, raiders were using rice beer and war drums to spur themselves for attack. The women sang and danced their praises for the bravery of their men in battle, heating the blood in the warriors' veins, as they anticipated a rich harvest of enemy heads.

Too soon, these erstwhile 'neighbours' rushed down a steep trail and up another mountainside to Molung, where they stole past the sentries and demolished the village gate. Too late the sentries raised the alarm. A diabolical war cry by the Tamlu marauders called forth the men of Molung to protect their village. Spears flew in all directions, as daos were lifted high to draw blood. The battle raged furiously, while Molung's old men pounded out the single ominous tone of the wooden war drums to alert neighbouring villages of potential attack. When defeat was obvious, Molung's women and children emerged from thatched dwellings to curse the invaders even as they begged for mercy, to no avail. Women were killed, but the children were captured and held for sacrifice to angry spirits. The terrified children ran past headless corpses along the village paths, but many were captured and dragged away to be offered as human sacrifices. In Molung, the blood ran in rivulets and soaked into the sandy soil. Even the animals cried out in terror, as the clamour of the battle echoed through the surrounding hills. In the end, these malicious invaders torched the thatched huts. Quickly, the village went up in flames and the smell of burning flesh permeated the night.

The warriors returned to Tamlu amid a tumult of welcome, as women rushed down the hill to throw themselves at the men's feet. They followed the men into the village, where they delivered the night's bounty, heads and captives, to the village elders. Then the gruesome task of cleaning skulls began. Old men and women delightedly immersed their hands in human blood, as the younger men, fired by this blood-lust, began their victory dances; admiring young women offered their bodies to the heroes. Huddled in fear, Molung's captured children cried for mercy, knowing their leg muscles would soon be cut, eliminating any possibility of escape. Later, they would be tortured during wild victory dances. Some would be trussed and lowered into a deep pit, where the post from outside the morung would be dropped on them, crushing their tender bodies. Other victims might be staked in a field before a scheduled burn. The victim would then watch as the fire moved closer, consuming him or her. The charred remains were then left in the field as a sacrifice for a bountiful harvest. Such was the life of the pagan Nagas: a grisly paradox of honour and horror. These otherwise kind and merry people terrorised one another in the mistaken pursuit of the spiritual powers they believed to reside in a person's head.

Children's heads taken in a raid

Such raids were unfortunately frequent enough among the Nagas that the Assamese people hated them and treated the people with distrust and fear when the Nagas came down from the hills to buy the few supplies they did not raise themselves. More importantly to my parents, the British government forbade their entry to any headhunting territory. However, in typical British bureaucratic rigmarole, they also warned that, should my parents ignore this decree, they should expect no British help if they were captured. Obviously, despite the chief's invitation in that first encounter, my parents were unable to respond to his request at that time.

My family's first home in the Naga Hills was in the bustling hill station of Kohima. The headquarters for the British government, Kohima also held the barracks and parade grounds of the Third Assam Rifles Regiment. The town had several old buildings and an attractive bungalow, which belonged to the British District Commissioner. There was also a bazaar with a few small shops. Above all this rose a steep hill where the mission compound nestled among the trees. It was here, on the 12th September 1929, that my sister Audrey was born.

The weather in Nagaland is quite mild - the average temperature being from a low in the mid fifties to a summertime high in the mid eighties. On the lower levels, the foliage is generally like a rainforest. Towering bamboo and huge ferns many feet tall line the roads, but the most impressive are the fantastic teak trees, whose leaves look to be as large as a beach umbrella.

Even higher than the compound stood the village that was the centre for the Angami tribe, with characteristic bamboo and thatched huts. Carved wooden wings and horns decorated the entrances - reminders of headhunting days. All the Nagas wore woven shawls that indicated their tribe; Angami shawls were generally white with a red stripe.

My family moved into a vacant bungalow, where my mother tried to set up housekeeping. They were now pukka missionaries - the real thing.

Assam Third Rifles on parade in Kohima

In the beginning, mother's limited knowledge of Assamese was a hindrance and my father often travelled his large territory for weeks at a time, giving my mother some anxiety about his health. But the weather was cool and pleasant and the people welcoming enough that they settled in, with their typical hard work and enthusiasm.

Dad was extremely busy with the Semas, as the work among them had increased the number of Christians to four thousand in sixty five villages, as well as having twenty two village schools with four hundred and fifty pupils that needed textbooks. He also started translation work in the Sema language. His health was good, even though he worked hard, but certain damages in my mother's body had to be repaired and so she returned to the Gauhati hospital for surgery. Dr Kinney and Dr Randall shared the operation and she passed the crisis, although she was very weak. While in the recovery room, a series of earthquakes occurred, which sent everybody running, not for cover, but for the open fields. She was too weak to be moved and, although the hospital building swayed and cracked, it did not collapse, but the succession of forty quakes from midnight till morning left her a nervous wreck.

I am glad our mission buildings were bolted together on rails, otherwise she would have been buried alive. She was still weak from her surgery and also suffered from frequent attacks of fever, perhaps due to malaria. It was here that my brother, Alford, was born. However, he soon died and is buried there.

Thanksgiving Day in 1930 was a bit dismal at our house. My father was on tour, all the children were sick, their food supply was low and very plain and my mother had no ambition to celebrate. When the Supplees, the other missionary family, came over to invite all of them to their home for Thanksgiving dinner, Mother was more than happy to accept. While she was getting ready to go to their home, half a mile away, who should come, but her husband, weary, soaked, sweaty and smelling of Naga smoke, but nevertheless welcomed with a hug. He hurriedly bathed while she found him some clean clothes. Her heart was filled with Thanksgiving.

Whenever Dad would return from a tour, he always managed to get Mother a fresh supply of fruit. Once in a while, they could order a basket of apples from Kashmir. This was a real treat. Occasionally, they also got some walnuts from the same garden, but these delicacies were too expensive to order more than once in a while.

In the winter of 1932, the family needed dental work done and planned for a trip to Calcutta, seven hundred miles away, which is an awful long trip to make if you have a severe toothache. By this time, they all began to feel in need of a furlough, as their workload had been extremely heavy for first termers and my mother's health had not been the best. They had been in India for six long years. The years had taken their toll on their zeal and they felt in need of renewal.

Disappointments are not unknown to missionaries and my mother's came when they were told to stay over because of the shortage of personnel and funds in the mission. They had been eager to let the children have the experience of being with their relatives and to know the land of which they were so proud. The conversation was spirited and alive when they talked about their furlough. When they were denied their right to a furlough according to the rules, their hearts were heavy, if not downright rebellious.

There was also another reason for my mother's eagerness to get home and find medical help. She was now looking for a baby boy to take the place of the one that was not permitted to live. To have her baby in the United States, where his life would be safe, was now her desire. But it was not to be. On the 10th June 1932, the baby was due to arrive and Dr Ahlquist, a missionary doctor, was back in India from furlough. He promised to see her through the ordeal. He also assured Mother that he would bring his nurse, to care for her. Mother's disappointment in having to be on the field rather than at home in the States, rankled her soul.

When a baby boy, who was named Bruce, was born and both she and the baby were alive, she was thankful to God, but the doctor, seeing her condition, ordered two weeks in bed. Mother's long convalescing period developed trouble in her legs, which added to her misery and also hindered her in the work when she did get in circulation once more. "The children needed me and my desire was to work for them and for nobody else." But life has a tendency to go on and time passes. A renewed request for furlough was finally granted after some delays and they were able to negotiate for a passage home, which they felt was long overdue.

6
THE FIRST FURLOUGH

As much as Mother wanted a furlough, she found it hard to leave Kohima and their temporary home. They were invited to the Supplees for their farewell meal and then George Supplee took them down to Manipur station. There they were met by the many friends who had come from Jorhat and Golaghat to see them on their way.

From Mother's diary: "This was a most unexpected and yet welcome gesture and my tears were a mixture of joy and sadness. It became very clear to me that 'a fellowship of kindred minds is like to that above'."

Mother was proud of being a part of that fellowship, which had often seemed to them to be stronger than that of flesh and blood. It had been a hard and long term of service for them, their bodies were weary and their minds depressed, but their hearts were lifted by these expressions of love and true companionship.

But it was not only the companionship with missionaries that made their life pleasant; they also had a very strong friendship with the Nagas and the Christian workers. As a friendly gesture on their part and recognition for faithful service, they had invited their Sema evangelist, Inaho, to accompany them to Calcutta and see the big city. He had never been out of Assam before and they knew that he wanted to go along.

My father was eager to see what this chief of the Semas would say and do in Calcutta. But Dad was disappointed at first, because Inaho did not seem impressed by anything my dad showed him of the glory in the metropolis. It was not until the day he was to board the train and return that he mentioned his desire to make some purchases before leaving them. Mother was curious to see what he wanted to buy. The two men went to the market and returned with their arms full of grape juice bottles. Mom had expected him to buy a dress for his wife, shoes for his children perhaps some gadget for himself or his home. Why grape juice? Mother knew even before he told them: after their departure, he would be responsible for giving the Lord's Supper to the Christians and that was to him most important. Who said that the native converts do not understand the meaning of the death of Christ? Mother shed a few tears again and then she found a suitcase (not the best one) emptied it and packed the bottles in it, so that he could transport them back to the Naga Hills without any breakage. When my dad took him to the train, Mother wept again. Now they could have communion service. The next morning, they boarded the ship and left the land of cows and crows.

The conduct of the passengers was a symbol of their philosophy of life: some drank in excess, others danced and flirted. When a few of them found a quiet corner, they would gather to pray for divine guidance as they travelled. Back in the States, my grandmother had written to my parents that my grandfather was not very well. Mother was concerned about her dear old dad. But her meditations were soon interrupted by her children who found so many interesting objects on board and by the crying of my brother, Bruce, who wanted her loving attention. He was then only seven months old. June was trying to continue her studies, but they soon decided to put the books away for the duration. There are so many things on board and in the water to see and also on shore, as they passed through the

Indian Ocean, the Singapore Straits, the South China Sea and into the Pacific. They did not lack for entertainment. Names that formerly had only been part of geography now became real to them: Rangoon, Penang, Kuala Lumpur, Singapore, Hong Kong, Shanghai, Kobe, Yokohama and Honolulu. What a time they had.

The SS President Hoover was a much better ship than the one they had boarded at Calcutta and they enjoyed the good food and the spacious cabins. One day, Mother almost lost her baby, Bruce. Another passenger had promised to look after him. This woman conveniently left that responsibility to five-year-old Audrey. Being too small to manage both him and the buggy, both came too near the stairway leading to the dining room. The baby buggy containing baby Bruce rolled down the stairs towards the dining room. Mother heard the commotion and ran to see what it was. A steward came carrying the baby and assured her that all was well. He then asked her to release the ship from all liabilities. Mother was too worried to do anything but make sure that the baby was not seriously injured. Poor sister Audrey felt even worse than Mother did, but it was not her fault, so Mother did not scold her.

Not long after this event, Mother once again had another scare. One of the immaculately dressed British stewards came to her. "Madam," he purred, "I do believe your eldest son is soon to fall overboard. You see, he has climbed over the ship's railing and is hanging outside the ship!" Rushing up on deck, she frantically retrieved the little rascal!

When they docked at Honolulu, a classmate of Dad's, Dr George Perre, came on board and welcomed them. He also brought a letter from Mother's brother, Albin, but since it was not from her mother, she did not take time to read it.

My first passport photo 1934. Jim, June, Audrey, Dad, Mother, Bruce and me

Mother saw the two men talking in a serious mood but she was busy getting the children ready to go ashore, so she paid slight attention to them. When they were driving around sightseeing, in the doctor's car, Mother asked Father for the letter, but he had forgotten to bring it. When Mother asked what was in it, he was evasive. It bothered her, but there were so many things to see that she was distracted. When they returned to the ship, mother immediately demanded to see the letter. She read it with a cry for mercy. Her mother had passed away and would not be there to welcome them home. After seven years of working for God, was this the reward? Mother was bitter, so she did not want to see anybody at home. She asked my dad to buy a return ticket at once and let her live out her life in India.

The sorrow overwhelmed her and her faith faltered. When they reached Minneapolis, her brothers and father were there to meet them and again the tears flowed. They reported that her mother was in a vault and would be interred after their arrival. It was a small comfort that Mother would at least have a last look at her face before the grave would claim her. Gradually, Mom came to realise that the life of a believer continues and that they would meet again in a better land. Her faith was being revived after a terrible struggle.

On the 11th November 1934, I came onto the scene. It all happened on the eleventh day of the eleventh month of the eleventh year of my parents' marriage. It was not an easy time for my mother. She came down, once again, with malaria and phlebitis. She had to remain in the hospital for six weeks. It was no problem for me, as I was cared for by my grandfather. I have always felt that my grandfather snuck some coffee in my baby bottle. (That would explain my addiction to coffee!) Poor granddad. My father had pneumonia and the older kids all had measles, so they couldn't help take care of me!

It was now 1935 and once again time to return to India...

The Journey To England (June, then age nine, remembers)

After saying good bye to our Minnesota relatives, we boarded the 'Hiawatha' streamliner in Saint Paul and eventually arrived in NYC. One last meeting with our

Foreign Missions Board and then the journey to England on the elegant SS Majestic, arriving a week later in Southampton. Since we had the largest family, we were assigned to a suite of 3 cabins. Imagine the thrill when, June, a 9 year old, had her own small cabin, probably meant for a nanny.

Our hotel in London was an older one and had no crib for baby sister Bea. So she had to sleep in a dresser drawer. Hot water for baths was obtained by dropping sixpence in the water heater. One day we visited Westminster Abbey and then did some shopping for more necessities in a large department store. Brother Jim got lost somewhere in the store. Eventually, he was found by the floor walker and was returned to us, safe and sound.

The Trip Back To India - October 1935 (June remembers)

On the 13th October 1935, we boarded the P&O liner 'Mulberra' in Liverpool and began the trip to India. Our cabin was small and crowded, so Jim and Dad were assigned a cabin across the hall.

As per English custom, children were expected to stay in the playroom with several nannies and not run around the deck. In the afternoon, the Americans decided to ignore this custom and two young Andersons went running down the halls, knocking on the doors of the napping English folks, Jim, pulling a rope with Audrey on the other end. The aroused English folks, on responding to the knock on the door, would emerge just in time to see this cute young 5 year old racing behind her big brother. Soon angry notes appeared on the bulletin board, telling the Americans to control their kids.

All dressed up for a masquerade party on board the "Mulberra"

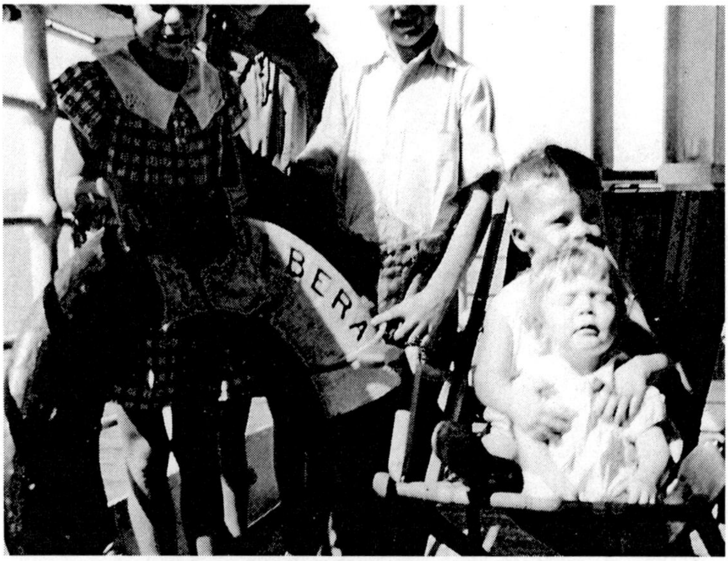

Brother Bruce helps me to relax on board ship

Life on shipboard

A variety of animals were on board, including ten horses, three dogs, one llama and several geese. The horses were going to Port Said to travel on to the war, in what is now known as Ethiopia. The rest were bound for India. One of the horses became ill and died. Its body had to be thrown overboard at night, when the passengers were asleep.

Port Said was fascinating and we went ashore to do some sightseeing. Many vendors came aboard to sell their wares. The Suez Canal was very hot in October. We also stopped at the port of Aden before proceeding to India.

After a stop in beautiful green Cochin, on the southwest coast of India, we sailed to Ceylon and spent a few days in Colombo, where Dad purchased a beautiful opal for Mother. Then we went up the coast with a one night stop at Visakhapatnam and on to Calcutta. We stayed at the Lee Memorial in Calcutta - a favorite inn for missionaries. India was the same as always: with crows, mynah birds, pye dogs and people sleeping on the sidewalks; we had returned to the land that we loved.

A few days of shopping for necessary items and we boarded the train for Gauhati, crossed the Brahmaputra on a ferry and proceeded to Jorhat. We arrived there for a missionary conference and got to visit our many friends.

Our Bungalow At Impur

Impur was where we were sent when we returned to India in 1935. It was a beautiful mission station with deep valleys, rugged mountains mixed in with the beautiful patchwork of rice fields, intermingled with the deep green of the jungle. Above the mission compound was the village of Mopungchukit and just below our yard were the school buildings and the teachers' houses. At this time, there was no church building. The old bungalow in which we were to live was not fit for occupation. The cloth ceilings were full of rats' nests. The floorboards were in terrible condition, with cracks big enough to let snakes in.

The bungalow in Impur before we renovated it

Jim and Audrey with Satcho

Imtisua, a faithful Naga carpenter and my father tackled the job of cleaning and repairing the old bungalow. Some of the schoolboys were recruited to chisel stone bricks from a huge rock found on the compound. These were used to build a fireplace to heat our home during the cold winter months, when the strong winds swept up the valley.

My Sister, Audrey, Remembers Our Bungalow At Impur

Our yard at Impur was large. Across our front yard was Dad's office. He worked hard there to do translation work and printing schoolbooks. Going down our front yard from our home was a long string of steps made of stone. Along these steps stood very tall palm trees and a huge evergreen tree. That tree was great fun to climb and a favourite of us kids. The teacher's children whom we played with had fun doing this and remember it well to this day. The teachers had homes just beyond our yard and some farther away.

In the garden stood the most huge and lovely bougainvillea tree. It was Mother's pride and joy. She also had a large area filled with rose bushes. They gave her the most gorgeous roses. Often, maybe every Sunday, she would have a vase full of them at church and in our home. One time, unfortunately, she was scratched on the top of her hand by a rose thorn and it became a staphylococcus infection. It would not heal and in the end she had to go to Calcutta, where they made a salve especially for her. It finally healed. We had a lot of fruit trees in this garden: oranges, pears, bananas, guavas and figs. Also, many vegetables that our gardener, Tekaleptan, did a good job of raising. At the entrance to this fenced-in garden was a trellis of honeysuckle and, at certain times of the year, it was full of sweet-smelling flowers.

We also had another garden on the road to our church. There we grew corn, fantastic blackberries and stinky cabbage. We kids loved exploring this huge garden. At the back of this garden grew a vine which had large, white trumpet-shaped blossoms. The Mali [gardener] told us that if we put one of these blossoms in our bedroom when we went to sleep at night and closed the windows and doors tight, by morning we would be dead! We never had the courage to try and prove him wrong!

We had a well for drinking water and washing, but during the winter months, we had to conserve on water as it was very dry. In the dry season, all our bath water was drained into a large metal tank under the bathroom and then used to water the garden. Our drinking water, which always had to be boiled, was carried by our 'pani-wallah' from a well quite a distance from the bungalow.

Our father had to almost completely re-model our home before we could live in it. It stood on chiselled stone blocks as foundation stones and was about three feet above ground. We would crawl under the house as kids and explore what was in the dirt - bugs, etc.

The front room was in the middle and on the east wall, there was a large, stone fireplace that my father had built. The dining room was towards the back of the house.

Our evenings were spent in quiet reflection in our living room, reading or playing games by kerosene lamps, as we had no electricity. Winter evenings were warmed by a roaring fire in the fireplace and hot water bottles were put in our beds, as we also had no central heating. The dining room was towards the back of the bungalow. Along the walls of the large dining room was a handsome built-in buffet that held Mother's fine china. An elegant kerosene chandelier hung above the dining room table and gave us the light we needed. In one corner of this dining room stood a small table with a pitcher of good drinking water in it for us.

Dinners at the Anderson home were truly elegant affairs, starting with the most delicious homemade soup, then probably chicken prepared in an Indian style, along with rice, vegetables, salad and the richest puddings or pies in life. Then somehow we found room for nuts, mints and/or akoi (popped rice). Dinner was always served by Nicheze, our bearer, in his starched white coat and pants. He wore a beautiful turban which proudly displayed a large brass 'A' on the front, for Anderson. The servants went home to their families in the village after dinner. Small wonder that we were reluctant to leave home for boarding school!

There was a long verandah across the back of the bungalow, with a covered walkway to a separate house, which was the cookhouse. This was where Shilo, our cook, prepared our meals on a large wood-burning cook-stove. Connected to that building was the dhobi's room, where Jongpong, our dhobi, washed and ironed all our clothes. He had to wash it all by hand. The white clothes were boiled in a large copper boiler. (Could this be because of our Swedish heritage? My father had often seen the very same technique used in rural Sweden).

Our living room was really two large rooms open in the middle, divided with a heavy curtain at each side. There were also curtains on a bay window out to our verandah. In this window was a teakwood table that folded up. We used it for tea in front of our fireplace in the winter months. Mother always had pretty flowers in a vase on this table.

Our fireplace was large and built of stones hand-cut by the schoolboys. Our servants would build a good fire here in the cold weather and we would love to get dressed each morning in front of the warm fire. We had a wind-up Victrola in this room and many old records, which we loved to listen to. The only lighting in our living room was one quite large kerosene lamp. In the evenings, Mom and Dad would sit close to it and read or sew as Mother made braided rugs. We would sit there, also near the fire and read books and encyclopaedias until bedtime.

June and I had a large bedroom and a half bath at one end of the house. Jim and Bruce had a bedroom near to Mom and Dad's at the other end of the house. Bea had to sleep in our parents' bedroom until she was older.

Our father had improvised a lovely bathroom in the bungalow. A large above-ground rainwater reservoir was built outside, with a water line and a tap that ran into a medium sized galvanised bathtub, which sat on 4x4" timbers to raise it off of the floor. This clever fresh water supply enabled us to also flush the toilet with a bucket. This water was heated over a wood fire in a little hut outside. Consequently, after our baths, we often smelled like smoked herring! Heat in the winter was from a kerosene stove about 3' tall and round. As I was drying from my bath one time, I stood too close to the stove, backed into it and burned my rump! Water for brushing our teeth was kept in a tall decanter in a cupboard in the bathroom. At times, the wee ants would get in it. They had to be ignored. More protein.

Down the hill from the house, near a large mango tree, a septic tank had been dug. One day our huge, red Brahma bull named Rongi, fell through the cover of this septic tank.

It took ten strong young boys, from the mission school, to rig ropes around him and pull him out! Our Mali had the unpleasant job of bathing Rongi. Needless to say, we didn't graze our cattle in that area any more!

There was a long verandah running the length of our home in the front. We used this for teatime and for us to play in during rainy weather. Afternoons, some girls from the mission school would sit there as Mother taught them to knit or embroider and sew. It was totally screened in, with a good roof. We loved to tip over our wicker furniture and make playhouses.

Brother Bruce with our dog, Fido, at Impur

In the back of our house was another smaller verandah, mainly used by our servants to wash our dishes, fill and clean all our kerosene lamps every day and where they sat to polish the brass decorative pieces from our home. There was a wee room off this verandah where their work supplies were stored or where huge bunches of bananas were often hung to ripen.

There was also a steep stairway from this room leading to our attic. In the attic was one small window and a large cupboard that held all the things that came from churches in the USA, called 'white cross goodies'. These things were used as gifts for the teachers or any Naga person in need. In the monsoon weather, our wet laundry was hung there to dry. One time, we kids watched our cat give birth to her kittens up there.

At the one end of the verandah was Mom's small bake room, with a cupboard, counter and kerosene stove. She had to make all of our bread, cookies, cakes etc. as there was no store or any place to go to buy these things. Flour and sugar were kept on a table that stood with its feet in small tins with kerosene in them, so that no bugs could crawl in. A wire cupboard called a doolie was for storing perishable food - no refrigerator, no electricity.

Also, a large storeroom was off the verandah. In this storeroom, we kept all our canned food that had been ordered from Calcutta once a year. It was called a godown and was always kept locked. When we had any dental work done in Calcutta, Mother would shop for canned food, soap etc. This she would do in an area called New Market. It was an enormous area under one roof, where you could purchase most anything. Fresh meat, vegetables and such we could either grow in our garden or purchase in the villages. We had several sheep and chickens which turned up on our table now and then.

Also, the walkway to our cookhouse ran from this verandah. This was made of wood and built up off the ground and was also covered. In this cookhouse was a large wood cook-stove where the cook, named Shilo, cooked our meals and baked Mother's bread in the hot wood fire. It was fun to go out there and look into the kettles and see what was for dinner. Of course, the cook did not like that.

Behind this cookhouse, Dad had a garage for his motorcycle and his tools. To the side of the cookhouse was a higher area of land built up with stones; rose bushes grew on the top edge. They were large and very full of small pink roses that smelled good. There were also clotheslines to hang out our washing in the nice weather. Above this, Dad made a playhouse for us kids. Bea and I seemed to take it over. We had our dolls and toy dishes and would raid our garden for fresh peas or some sort of thing to eat from these play dishes - often mulberries from a nearby tree. The Naga girls would have fun with us up there. Jim and Bruce built their own playhouse and had their fun in that. Behind this area was a very large bamboo grove, where huge ficus or rubber trees grew. We did have fun climbing these big trees and marching through 8' tall elephant grass. We had no fear of the spiders or snakes that also made their homes there.

Next to Dad's garage was a chicken coop. We had many chickens as we ate them and counted on them for eggs. The Nagas that visited us from outlying villages would always bring us chickens. It was always fun to go and check on them. We held them in our arms like pets. Dad had a gun, as, at times, huge hawks would come around to try to catch these chickens. Next around the back of our house was a huge old, old barn; it was full of pieces of wood and junk. What a fantastic place to explore. There were doves in a homemade nest box and they were fun to watch. Also, many pumpkins that had been purchased from the villagers were stored in a room there, along with a big basket of cottonseeds. These were cooked for our cows along with rice. This was done in the same shed where our water was heated for bathing. This mash was cooked, cooled and fed to our cattle in the evenings. It would be poured into a wooden feed bin from which they would eat.

A current photo of the church Dad built in Impur

The mission church in Impur was built on a beautiful knoll overlooking the entire mission compound. It was a lovely church, complete with a steeple and a bell. On Sundays we were all made to go to church and behave! Occasionally, June and Mother would sing a duet or June would play a lovely solo on the old pump organ. The Nagas absolutely love music and they especially love to sing. When they sing, their harmony sounds almost Polynesian.

Our barn was not far from our church, maybe one mile from our home. We would go over to this barn to help scrape off large leeches and ticks that were feasting on the cows' blood after a day's grazing out in the jungle. On one occasion, one of our horses had been sneezing for several days. We soon realised that he had a large leech up his nostril. Dad told our syce [groom] to withhold the horse's water for several days. When we finally gave him a bucket of water, we seasoned it with salt. What a shock when a four inch long hammerhead leech dropped into the bucket!

There was a large shed where wood was cut up for the stove and fireplace. I recall one day a man who was cutting up this wood missed the log and cut into the top of his foot. Mother had to put her nursing skills to use and mend his foot.

7
MY EARLIEST MEMORIES OF INDIA

My earliest recollections of my life in the Naga Hills of India begin in about 1939, or when I was five years old. I had the good fortune to be born into a large family with equally large amounts of love and love of life and adventure. By this time, my father and mother knew Assam well and to them it was home.

Father Bengt

My father was a tall, lanky Swede who, as a child, had rickets as a result of malnutrition. He was illegitimate and not until late in life did he know who his father was. He was put to work at a very early age. When he was seven, he would have to work in the forest with the lumber men. One time, he was cut on his leg quite severely. "Go pee on the cut," he was told. It was the old Swedish remedy. His childhood in Sweden was not an easy one. Bengt emigrated to America in 1915.

Mother Edna

Edna Michaelson Anderson was born to a large family in Alexandria, Minnesota. Her parents, who emigrated from Sweden, had a farm and later a hotel in this small Minnesota town. They never spoke much English. She had a bawdy sense of humor which matched her red hair. How she could live such a lonely, difficult life and maintain a love for India and its people is amazing. No real friends, no medical help within three days' journey, mail (if we were lucky) one day a week, no electricity, no running water and five wild – no, four wild, one sweet - children. She was an amazing woman.

Sister June
A red-haired, sweet, perfect little angel who never got dirty and never angry. When she is in India, she gets Delhi belly, throwing up and barely making a sound. Jim calls her Princess Snowflake. Her tombstone should have five snowflakes, because she has always been as pure as the driven snow.

Brother Jim
Jim was known to all my friends as the Swedish Crocodile Dundee. However, he looks exactly like a British tea planter. Could it be that when Dad was gone...? No, no... Well, never mind... He has a wicked sense of humour. What other old sucker goes to a gynaecologist for a physical! Thank God, he can't run for US president as he was born in India.

Sister Audrey
Audrey is so totally sweet. She's a total Mother Earth with more children, grandchildren and great-grandchildren than anyone I know!

Brother Bruce
Bruce was a sweet, melancholy redhead, with a raging temper to match that of the Vikings. They did get to Ireland, you know. He loved romance, whether it be in life or song. We lost him much too soon. He loved India and had a dream to be in the diplomatic service.

Two children never made it. The first being born in

North Dakota and the second, a boy named Alford, who died at birth in India.

All cleaned up for tea time under the guidance of my ayah, Tsungkumla

Tsungkumla, age 89, on my last visit to Nagaland

We had many Naga friends because there were no other Americans or Europeans living in our area. We conversed with these friends in Assamese, the provincial language of the state of Assam. I had a very wonderful nanny, (ayah) who was an Ao Naga. Her name was Tsungkumla. She was with me all day, every day, until I was six years of age. She saved me from several threats, such as when I reached to pull on a pretty green snake that hung from a palm tree in our front yard.

I spoke fluent Ao Naga, taught to me by my ayah. I do not recall much of this language. I do, however, remember speaking and thinking in Assamese - a dialect of Hindi, I think! This we all spoke to the servants and workers on our compound. Often my parents spoke Swedish to each other, but spoke only English with us.

Dad built us a wonderful playhouse, far enough away from the main house so that our noise couldn't be heard. We each had dear friends among the Naga teachers' children. We spent hours up there happily playing house and when we were older, trying to smoke old leaves in Naga pipes that had been given to our father. Amazingly enough, no one heard us choking and coughing.

We had cows that were kept mainly for milk. Boys from the school would be recruited to go into the jungle and cut grass for the horses and cows to eat. All of our animals were brought into the barn for the night, due to the many hungry tigers and leopards that came out of the jungle after dark!

Our horses, which we used for travel, were actually hill ponies. They were extremely sure-footed and quite small. In addition to horses, we had sheep, cows and chickens. The sheep were used for wool and meat. The Mali and the syce, who cared for our horses, would shear the sheep. Mother would wash the wool and then have girls from the mission school card it. She then made patchwork quilts and gave them to families who lived on the mission compound. As our meat supply was limited to chicken, occasionally we would slaughter one of the sheep for meat. Occasionally, the Nagas would bring us a wild boar that they had killed. The meat from these very ugly creatures was delicious.

I loved to play with our sweet little lambs

One of Dad's Sema Naga evangelists had borrowed Dad's gun to hunt for wild boar. Along with some men from the village, they camped in a rice field to wait for their chance, as the boar usually came out at night to raid the rice fields. That night, getting impatient, the Sema went into the jungle to look for the animal. Within minutes, a huge boar, with enormous tusks, lunged at him, tearing open the man's abdomen. Hearing his screams, the other hunters ran to his rescue. Several days later, realising that they could not help the man, they brought him to Mother, hoping that she could save the poor man's life. In horror, she saw that the villagers had pinned his intestines together with safety pins and made an attempt to sew him back up with ordinary needle and thread. Since there was nothing that she could do to help him, she was extremely upset. Of course, the poor man died.

Besides Mother's work as teacher, breadmaker and housekeeper, she was also nurse for her family and for the school. To purchase supplies, we had to order them from firms in Calcutta or from the bazaar in Jorhat. Eggs and chickens we could get from the Naga villagers, also rice and sometimes fish. Baking bread was her job as there was no baker. We ordered flour from Jorhat; yeast she made from her own recipe, using rice beer and hops as a starter.

To get milk was our biggest problem. The Nagas did not milk their cows and did not use milk, except when a mother died and left a hungry infant. One day, Dad read that the Viceroy of India was eager to improve the cattle in the villages. When Dad asked the Deputy Commissioner for advice, he told him to contact a tea planter to see if he could spare one of his purebred herd. He was willing to part with a young bull. After further correspondence, two sturdy dependable Nagas went down to the plantation and took delivery.

Bogey - our precious supplier of milk

Jim and Bruce with Bogey's calf

My fifth birthday party

My dear friend "Fido" keeping me safe by our bungalow

The young animal was not favourably inclined to follow the two strangers. The angry young bull took off after them and sent them scampering up the nearest tree. The manager and his men must have seen a jolly good show, watching the whole performance. However, that did not end it. The kind-hearted gentleman decided that he would not disappoint us children who needed the milk, so he selected a young heifer to serve as a consort to the obstinate male. The welcome that the two animals received was most elaborate - not only at first, but even more so when calves arrived and became the objects of special care and attention. We now had sufficient milk, not only for the family, but we could also share it with babies in homes where the mother had died. Eternal vigilance was the price we paid. Local tigers had an eye on the plump specimens of pure Brahma stock. Needless to say, we kept the barn door well-locked at night.

Our Daily Chores

Our days were mostly glorious events of exploring and learning about the terrain and wildlife in the Naga Hills. Weekday mornings we would rise at approximately 7:00am with a tray of tea and cookies by our bedside. This was called palang chai.

School was in a room at one end of our bungalow and consisted of Mother teaching us the Calvert course, which was sent out from the USA. We breezed through our assignments and were out in the yard to play by 11:30am. Actually, Mother was, by that time, eager to be rid of us. Tiffin was served around noon, after which we took naps and were up and about to ride the horses or play croquet until 4:00pm, at which time we had tea on the front verandah which overlooked the garden.

Tea was a high point of the day and it was a relaxing time to talk over the events of the day. The fine china and linens were used, cucumber or sardine sandwiches, along with olives, cakes and cookies and positively the most delicious tea in the whole world, grown right in our beautiful Assam.

Mission compound at Impur

When one of us had a birthday, Mother would give great parties for fifteen to twenty children. We would have party favours, paper hats and a delicious birthday cake. All our Naga friends would arrive at the party scrubbed clean and wearing fresh clothes. Our presents were always toys and things purchased from Calcutta or clothes that Mother had secretly made for us. The Naga children were thrilled to be included in the parties, but seemed ill at ease and not used to eating with Western utensils.

One afternoon, all five of us children were washed and out in our front yard, waiting for tea to be served. Suddenly, we saw Mayang, my Dad's assistant running towards us with a long stick in his hand. We thought he had gone mad, then we saw a nine foot long black viper headed across the lawn towards us. Catching up with the snake, Mayang swiftly beat it to death. It transpired that while he was working on a hymn book translation with Dad in his office, he looked out the window and saw the snake headed for us. Dad's office was in a far corner of our large yard. We were extremely grateful to Mayang.

Our bungalow and the surrounding compound were situated on a hill. Many times, pregnant women from the village would dig out the soil under Dad's office, undermining the building. They would fill up their baskets with this dirt which they would then eat. Perhaps this was due to a mineral deficiency in their systems.

At times, large flying termites would come out of the ground. The Naga children would collect them and eat them. The Naga diet consisted mainly of a red-coloured rice, some greens and pork. Due to the fact that the local pigs also acted as the sewage treatment plant, we never ate pork, only wild boar. Other Naga delicacies were bright green stink beetles and enormous red spiders with shiny black legs. I once asked a playmate what they tasted like. Her reply was, "very spicy".

Tekaleptan, our Mali (gardener)

Afternoon tea on the lawn

One of our favorite pastimes was to hang out with our Mali. His name was Tekaleptan. He was a short, stocky man who wore only a grubby loin cloth and a homespun Naga shawl around his shoulders. On his buttocks, he had tied a wooden block with a slot in it; here he carried his dao. He had a large black callus on each hip from sleeping on a dirt floor in his native hut.

Often, we would search the garden for a large, round hole lined with a silky web. This was the home of a tarantula. When we found one we would coerce the Mali into hunting the poor creature. To do this, he would sharpen a long piece of bamboo. Taking his dao he would slowly cut away the earth around the hole, all the while keeping his sharpened bamboo poised for the kill!

We had a great time ridding the garden of these frightening creatures, but unfortunately it all came to a screeching halt when brother Bruce decided to terrify

Mother and brought one of the impaled tarantulas onto the verandah. He carefully put the creepy spider down. Almost instantly, its big hairy legs began to thrash about in an effort to get away. At this point, Mother was so frightened that she almost had a heart attack! As a result, our tarantula hunting days were over.

The Mali's wife had almost died from a bite on her hand from a tarantula. Apparently, when she had been cultivating a field she must have disturbed the tarantula which then bit her on the hand. Her son quickly took his dao, made a cut and sucked out the poison.

Another favorite distraction for us was to play with the Naga spears that had been given to Dad by the natives. These lances were quite deadly as they had actually been used by the Nagas for hunting. We would each take a spear and head for the lower part of the garden where the banana trees grew. This way, we would be out of the sight of our parents. Pretending that the banana trees were killer tigers, we would give out a fierce yell and throw our spears at them. Being a total brat, I wanted to do something different, so just as Jim threw his spear, I stuck my leg out and caught the spear right in the calf. Of course, this ended another one of our favourite pastimes. Some serious scolding from Dad and some comforting medical attention from Mother soon put things right again. Nevertheless, prowling the bamboo patch remained a pretty exciting thing to do.

The Naga Hills were home to many bears. Brother Jim recalls an incident that occurred near our village:

"On one occasion, two Naga men were out in the jungle, cutting wood. An aggressive bear came by and, in desperation, one man started to climb a tree, with the hungry bear right behind him. The man on the ground jumped as high as he could and, with a strong blow of his dao, cut off one of the bear's hind legs. The bear fell to the ground, roaring and screaming in agony. The tree climber jumped down to help. In the ensuing struggle - a fierce fight it was indeed - the bear was killed, but not before it tore off the right side of one man's face, among other injuries. The men returned to the village, but no amount of first aid could close the gaping wound in his face. It was decided that he should be taken to see the memsahib, who could heal all sickness.

"When he arrived in Impur, there was little that Mother could do, except cut away and sterilise some of the loose tissue. There was no sign of infection, as maggots had eaten away the dead tissue to the bone and probably saved his life.

"Forever after, he had to hold his hand to his cheek to keep the food from falling out, Mother said. Only June was permitted to see this man; the rest of us were too young."

In our yard, we had several large oak trees. There were huge wasps several inches long, brown with huge yellow heads. These were called tarantula wasps and they ate the fermented sap from these trees. One stung Jim! One of the teachers in the mission school made a cut and sucked out the venom, saving his life! He remained in a critical condition for several days as a result of this. During the monsoon season, which ran from June until September, we were plagued with leeches. Often we would get terrible infections from the leeches. We called them Naga sores. It would take weeks for them to heal.

Assam and Nagaland are also famous for earthquakes, our family having experienced some of great magnitude. In the event of an earthquake, should one occur after dusk, there would be a mad scramble to turn off all the kerosene lamps, thus preventing a fire. Some of these earthquakes were so violent, we often felt as if we were going to be thrown off the mountain. I remember as a child, clinging to the grass in fear. We did usually get a warning, as all of the local dogs, including our black Labrador, Fido (yes, that was his name), would start to howl several minutes before the shaking started.

On many occasions, fires would roar up the mountainside, burning many a village. This was due to the slash and burn method of preparing the fields for planting. Trees would be cut down and then burned, along with all surrounding brush. All it took was for a few burning branches to be blown up the hill to the village and to where the thatched roof houses were. In a matter of minutes, the entire village would go up in flames. Whether we were experiencing earthquakes, fires, life-threatening critters or tropical diseases, life was never dull. It was a marvellous education.

Art and Craft of the Nagas

The Nagas have a rich tradition of art and crafts, rooted in a lifestyle that has always been in harmony with the environment they live in. They weave their own cloth from home spun cotton which is grown in their fields. The art of weaving is popular among the Naga women and the colorful shawls and bags woven by them are extremely beautiful. Each tribe uses distinguishing colours and motifs that are often based on tribal folklore. Earlier, natural dyes extracted from tree bark, roots and plants were used for dyeing cotton yarn and woven fabrics. In addition, the woven cloth was embellished with beads, cowrie shells and goat's hair to denote the wealth and status of the person wearing the shawl. Many symbolise head-taking.

Pottery was known to the early Nagas and is still mostly done by the womenfolk. The clay pots made are generally very simple and importance is given to their functional value, rather than aesthetics. Naga storage baskets were woven by women using fine strips of cane and bamboo.

Nagas are excellent woodcarvers, making use of simple rudimentary tools and implements such as the dao. Skilled craftsmen produce great works of art that adorn village gates and house posts, as well as objects of utility like the common wooden dish. Iron, tin and brass were used to produce weapons such as the dao, as well items of utility and ornaments. The Konyak blacksmiths were famous for their work in the early days and their products were in great demand on the plains of Assam.

The colour and beauty of the traditional shawl or blanket symbolise the wealth and status of the wearer, as well as the skill of the maker. The abundance of raw materials, the splendid environment and the inherent skills of the people have all played a role in generating a rich history in Nagaland.

Gourmet Dining in Nagaland

The Nagas like hunting and fishing. It is the 'wizard' of every village who is asked about good fishing. If he is given a few pigs or goats, he will let you know which day is best for fishing. The Nagas have the belief that women will ruin good fishing. Therefore, no women were allowed to join in any fishing trip. The men would throw big stones and trees into the wild river to begin building a dam. This work would normally take a few hours. During this process, some of the boys and men would crush poisonous fruit and then place them in braided baskets. They would then tie the baskets to bamboo poles in the water. After a few minutes, the poison would spread and the boys and men could start picking up the floating fish. Usually the poison only affected the fish - that is, if they used the right kind of poisonous fruit. Sometimes, they would use stronger poison that could affect their own health.

One time, we were given a large fish by the natives from the village. Fish was really considered a luxury, so we were thrilled to have some. Unknown to us, the natives had killed the fish with poison! Of course, we all became deathly ill - Mother was furious. Thankfully, we all survived.

When the Naga men would come to visit my father, they would often bring us chickens as gifts, so we always had a good supply of chicken to eat. I had a pet rooster named 'Easy'. He had earned his name because he was very easy to catch! He was a beautiful black and white bird. Unfortunately, without my knowledge, he became a chicken dinner one evening! Early the next morning, when I went out to feed the chickens and collect eggs, Easy was nowhere to be seen! Expecting the worst, I confronted Shilo, the cook and he confirmed my dreaded fears! I was devastated, I was mad and I was deeply hurt! I felt that I had lost a good friend. Shilo was no longer on my A-list!

The Roads and Our Travels in the Naga Hills

The roads in the Naga Hills were extremely primitive, as they had been built mainly for people travelling on foot. They generally ran along the side of a mountain. Most of our travel was done on horseback, but when we were very small, we were carried on the backs of coolies. We had a great hooded chair made out of wicker that I would sit in and a coolie would carry it on his back with a strap on his head. Later on, Mother and Dad had a huge Harley-Davidson motorcycle which they used for travel.

Travel in the Naga hills

Dad and Jim with June on the pony in a "ring" saddle

Dad and Mother on their Harley-Davidson motorcycle

Bruce and me with some dear friends

A Brand New Harley-Davidson

A Fergus Falls, Minnesota church donated a brand new Harley-Davidson to my father. The motorcycle arrived in Calcutta and became a great help in his touring program. The main trails were wide enough for the bike, but bridges were a problem, as they were narrow between the railings and if made from bamboo, they were not always safe for a heavy vehicle. Occasionally, landslides would obstruct his path and then at other times when the path would be slippery, he would take a spill. Sometimes the after-effects were not so pleasant, since the path was rough and the travel tedious, but injuries sustained were never fatal. Twice, however, he might have been killed when he lost control of the powerful motorcycle and it landed on top of him. At other times, it developed mechanical trouble and Dad had to leave it in a far-off village and walk home.

He was a tough old Swede, as was my mother. Once while they were touring the Naga Hills on Dad's big Harley-Davidson, Dad was explaining to Mother the flora and fauna that grew on the mountainside, as he knew how fond she was of the native plants. He soon realised that he was getting no response from her. Looking over his shoulder he panicked when, he saw that she was not on the back seat. Turning the big bike around, he drove as fast as the trail would permit. Rounding a bend there he found her sitting on the ground laughing. Later, she admitted that she had been quite afraid because of the strange sounds that were coming out of the nearby jungle.

On one occasion, his big bike slid out from under him and he dropped thirty feet. He heard some Nagas working in a field nearby. He was in terrible pain, but summoned the strength to call to them for help. With the use of their daos, they cut a path and pushed the heavy bike back up to the road. After strapping his belt around his extremely painful hips, he got back on the bike and completed his journey to a village where he worked for three days. Sometime later, he was told by the mission doctor that he had suffered a separated pelvis. He was a tough old Swede.

Later on, during World War Two, my father was given a Jeep by the American soldiers based in Jorhat. He truly appreciated this new mode of transportation. However, it was much more dangerous with the Jeep than it had been with the motorcycle to drive on those narrow mountain roads, with twenty-six switchbacks between Jorhat and home. It was on one of these switchbacks where Dad, one of our servants and I crashed while attempting to make several turns.

The brakes failed and the Jeep dropped fifty feet, landing on its side. The servant and I jumped clear, but Dad was still inside the Jeep. I rushed to the Jeep and found him unconscious. A small tree had kept the vehicle from rolling on top of him. I turned off the ignition and, using all the strength of my fourteen years, pulled him out of the Jeep. Once he regained consciousness, he sent the servant running to the nearby village to recruit men to once again cut a path and push the Jeep back on the road. I had to walk behind the Jeep carrying a large stone to quickly put behind the rear wheel in case the brakes failed again. This was what my dad called 'The Swedish Emergency Brake'.

Later we were given a WWII jeep, a gift from the American GIs stationed at Jorhat

Part of Dad's missionary work was to travel to the villages of his territory, which included several different Naga tribes. This travel we called 'Mofussil'. On occasion, we would all travel with him. There were seven of us, so this was no easy task, but for us children it was very exciting. All of our clothes for the trip would be packed in trunks. Dishes and cooking utensils went in a "Japha" - a large round basket. Bedding was packed in bed rolls and food in wooden boxes. All of this was carried on the backs of coolies. Meanwhile, the syce had the horses saddled up and ready for us children. Tied to each saddle was a small bag of oranges, which we would devour with much enthusiasm as we got thirsty on the trip. Several of the servants would carry our lunches in tiffin baskets. Lunch usually consisted of several pieces of cold chicken, buttered homemade bread and cookies.

It was on a road in this jungle, several years later, that Mr Adams, the District Commissioner, and his bride were travelling to come and visit us. They journeyed with a contingent of Gurkha sepoys and three cocker spaniels. Stopping along the road to rest, a leopard suddenly dropped from a tree above them, snatched one of the dogs and vanished into the jungle before any of the sepoys could reach their guns.

On one trip, while our family was visiting a remote village on the headhunting border, none of the coolies who were to carry our supplies showed up. It was rice-harvesting season and the only men available were from a village across the border in headhunting country. In my enthusiasm to get underway, I ran into my travel chair and strapped myself in. Recognising a pretty light load, one of the headhunters strapped my chair to his head and headed off to the next village. My parents were panicked, but happy when they finally arrived there and I ran to greet them.

During the heavy monsoons, Dad wanted to visit a village in the headhunting country of the very primitive Yimchunger tribe. The road was impassable for the motorcycle, so he travelled by horse and arrived at the village after a tiring three-day trip in the rain. Once camp was set up and after proper greetings to the village chief and elders, he noticed two naturally beautiful girls, standing by the chief who said:

"It is my honour to offer you my daughters to comfort you through the night after so long a journey. It is also the custom for important men visiting my village to bring the chief gifts of tobacco, whiskey and a red blanket. In return, I will share my daughters with them".

"I appreciate your generosity," said my father, "but my people believe no good can result from this custom. It is a sin, it is wrong, I cannot accept your offer."

The chief, with an angry look in his eyes, said, "I know not what is a sin, I know not what is wrong. I do know that this is good." Soon it was time for Dad to leave. He was packed up and waiting for the horse. No horse. He went to the chief standing in front of his house, which was decorated with a dozen or so human skulls and enquired after the horse. "You don't like my daughters, I don't like your horse. My men have eaten it". So Dad, with an extra coolie carrying the saddle and bridle, had to walk home three days in the rain.

The year was 1940, I was six years old and India was my home. How I did love it! As far as I was concerned, there was no other place on Earth! On a camping trip to a nearby river, we travelled down a narrow hairpin trail that twisted and turned as it meandered down the mountainside. Where it neared the river, at the bottom, the dark green rainforest closed in like a vast emerald sanctuary.

Giant rubber trees mingled with bamboo. Tall graceful palms made shadows on a carpet of pale green ferns which covered the valley floor. The horses nickered in anticipation of a much-needed rest and a cool drink of water with which to quench their thirst. They were actually a breed of small, Indian hill ponies. We only had three of them with us on this trip, so my family had to take turns riding.

Suddenly, we saw a crowd of Nagas. There were men, women and young children. The boys and men were cutting down trees and bushes. The women and girls were collecting the branches and sticks in large piles for firewood. This type of work was extremely dangerous. The bushes had sharp thorns and, on the ground, there were poisonous snakes and scorpions lurking. The air was buzzing with dangerous mosquitoes.

Worst of all were the horrible, blood-sucking leeches, crawling everywhere, on the ground or in the trees and bushes by the thousands, waiting to feast on the naked, sweaty, human bodies. It was a strenuous job to convert the jungle into fields for farming, which was their main source of living.

As we entered the damp, pungent darkness of the jungle, Rhesus monkeys shrieked an alarm and leapt from limb to limb, startling the birds. A pair of gigantic hornbills terrified us, as they clacked their enormous beaks in fright and flew deeper into the shadows. Orchids hung from tree branches in heavy clusters of ivory, coral and brilliant yellow. The sweet scent of wild ginger blossoms perfumed the air.

The narrow path was soft and spongy under the horses' hooves, due to a thick carpet of dead leaves and some of the greenest moss I had ever seen. Wild violets and Jack-in-the-Pulpit grew everywhere. Fat, orange toadstools stood like sentinels under the enormous trees that shielded the delicate life below. Their leaves allowed just the correct amount of sunlight through. Suddenly, the jungle became quiet, except for the squeaking of the leather on our saddles and the occasional hammering sound of a coppersmith bird. Our horses seemed anxious.

Soon we heard the distant roar of the river as it raced over the enormous boulders, growing as it sped down the valley, fed by numerous streams further up the mountains.

Turning to our syce, Tamang, my brother, Jim, shouted to be heard over the roar, "Do you think it's too swift to cross here?" he asked in Assamese.

"Oh yes," the Naga man yelled back. "We must follow the river some miles south before we can cross. It's much too dangerous right here." At that moment, I recalled how every year, just after the monsoon season, many lives were lost by Nagas attempting to cross these roaring rivers on foot.

Reining in our horses, we turned south along the riverbank, threading our way around fallen trees and slick boulders.

As I was sitting on my horse, my thoughts were wandering to the poor young boys, who were forced to guard the fields at night - the youngest one, not older than myself. Their lookout point was a small bamboo tower, which would give them a better view of the rice fields. Their mission was to scare off the elephant herds, by pounding on empty metal cans with anything, to make as much noise as possible. They didn't want the elephants to come and ruin their hard work, by trampling and destroying the fields. However, the elephants, snakes or tigers were not the biggest danger to the boys. What they feared the most were the leopards. These sneaky animals could easily and without a sound move around in the fields. If they wanted to stay alive, the boys really had to be on guard and not drift off to sleep, even for a short time. I heard the adults telling stories about how leopards had taken young boys and eaten them - even entering houses in the village to take sleeping children.

Rounding a bend in the river, we came upon a most welcome sight. There before us lay an expansive, crystal clear pool of quiet water. The jungle was on one side and to the west, up an embankment, was a wide open meadow, which at one time had been a rice field. "Here we will set up the tents," my father announced in an official voice. Farther down the river, to the south, was a rickety suspension bridge, "Not safe enough for people or horses," according to Father. In no time at all, all three tents had been set up. The largest one was for my mother and father and was the closest to the river. It had three screened windows and a porch. My brothers' tent was a small khaki-coloured one, while my two older sisters and I had a lovely off-white one. Before long, inside each tent, our beds were laid out on small canvas and wood camp cots. Bed rolls were laid neatly out, adding a feel of luxury. Folding chairs, tables and kerosene lamps, all in their places, made it complete. I loved the cosy tents and the clean smell of the canvas.

Toilet facilities consisted of a white enamel dishpan perched on top of a pedestal made of branches. Alongside was a bucket of water fetched from the river. This was for washing only, as all drinking water had to be boiled.

Heading to our campsite by the river with three of our helpers

Coolies with our camping gear

Camping by the river "Dikku Pani"

Our cook Shilo, his helper, Jim, June, Audrey, me, Mother, Bruce and Fido. A visit to one of the villages

Dad's "home" away from home

The Naga coolies, who had carried in all of our supplies, also dug a hole in the ground some distance from camp. Around this hole was placed a large bamboo mat in a circular, upright position. This was to be our latrine. The bamboo mat provided the necessary privacy. To be without electricity and running water at this point of my life was completely natural and was all I knew. It was wonderful to live this close to nature. Living, as we did, so far from civilisation, it has always amazed me how much we all learned to improvise. For instance, I remember our father making engine gaskets for our Jeep from the tanned skins of sheep.

Meanwhile, the servants had set up our 'dining room'. Four bamboo posts cut from the jungle held up a roof constructed from palm fronds. It gave it a nice airy feeling.

A folding table, chairs and a Coleman lantern completed the decor. Cooking was done on the ground on stones. Several equal-sized stones were brought from the river and they made up the burners. Wood from the jungle made up the fuel.

Shilo, our cook, was so amazing that he could make the most delicious chocolate pie, using an empty five gallon tea tin for an oven. When all was set up and looking complete, the coolies, who had carried all of our supplies into camp on their bare backs, were paid and sent back to their village, which was about fifteen miles away. Whenever we travelled in the Naga Hills, all of our supplies had to be transported in this manner. Occasionally, fresh vegetables, rice, live chickens and some very dubious eggs could be purchased from the villagers along the way. Most often, we brought all necessary items with us.

Remaining with us at the campsite were our cook, a bearer, plus my father's right-hand man, Kijung. Kijung worked in Impur with my father. He did everything, from translation of the Bible to taking charge of Dad's shotgun when we travelled.

Served on Mother's fine china was a delicious dinner of fresh fish, which we had caught while camp was being set up, coffee for my parents and hot chocolate for us children. Afterwards, it was off to bed, each to our respective tents, Mother and Father to read, Jim and Bruce to construct slingshots from branches they had cut during the day and us girls to huddle together in icy fear of all the predators that we knew existed just feet from our tent.

I always felt more secure when June and Audrey were home from the boarding school they attended in Darjeeling. Even so, sleep did not come quickly, especially when the sound of an owl hooting or a servant coughing became a tiger on the prowl in our vivid imaginations. Never would any one of us girls venture out to the latrine alone at night. Consequently, the Anderson girls had a bladder capacity quite like that of an elephant.

This fear, or maybe I should say 'respect', for the Indian wildlife had been augmented by a true story told to us by a friend of my father. It seems that their family had been spending the night at one of many dak bungalows, or rest houses, scattered throughout the British territory of Assam. The particular one that our friends were staying in had the toilet facilities located seventy-seven steps down a steep embankment. I know because we had stayed at this bungalow many times and I had counted them.

Very late one night, Albert, their son, answering the call of nature, flashlight in hand, headed bravely down those seventy-seven steps. A little over halfway down, he heard soft footsteps closing in behind him. Turning to see who was following him, he screamed in fright as the beam of his flashlight shone in the bright yellow eyes of an enormous leopard. Dashing into the toilet and slamming the heavy door behind him, he sat in absolute terror while the leopard slowly walked around and around the building, stopping occasionally to sniff at the door and smack its lips in anticipation of a tasty dinner. Luckily for Albert, the outhouse was constructed of very sturdy wood and stone.

The cooling "Dikku Pani." June, Audrey, me and Jim

The beautiful Menkong jungle across the valley from our home in Impur

Poor Albert screamed for hours to no avail, but no one in the main house could hear him. Terrified, he remained there until morning, when, totally exhausted, he climbed back up those seventy-seven steps. No, we would never venture out of our tent after dark!

The following morning dawned bright and clear at our campsite. After gulping down a delicious breakfast, we all bounded down to the river bank, where we found three rafts which the servants had built for us before we were up. They were constructed out of several lengths of bamboo which had been lashed together with thin vines. We had a marvellous time floating with the gentle current that flowed through our quiet part of the river. When the current was too slow, we would pole our rafts along in silly races, often tipping them over. Another favourite pastime was digging in the shallows among the rocks, looking for quartz. By the end of the day, we were dirty, wet and tired, but extremely happy.

Darkness falls quickly in the jungle, almost as if someone pulls down a shade. Once again, after dinner, horses fed and watered, people bedded down and the sounds of night in the jungle took over. From our tent, we could hear the servants talking in low, hushed tones as they sat by the fire to keep it going all night.

Around midnight, we were awakened by the voice of Kijung and the syce, calling softly, "Sahib, sahib, come quickly: bagheera [tiger]. I think he wants to eat the horses." We froze in our beds. This was it! The end was near. Then we heard the tiger roar! I have never been so afraid! We realised the thin canvas of our tent offered no protection from the beast!

Before long, we heard my father say to Kijung, "Here are

the gun and the bullets. Be sure not to merely wound it. That would be more dangerous than anything." By the time the second shot resounded across the valley, I'm sure that not a creature remained for miles around. Those were the loudest shots we had ever heard. Thank God that the horses were tethered or they would have taken off for home.

"Did you get it?" my father shouted. "No Sahib, I am afraid I missed, but we will keep watch!" answered Kijung. Sleep was slow to come after all that excitement and we were more than thankful when the sun finally crept over the mountain top.

A runner was sent to the nearest village to hire coolies, as our adventurous weekend trip had come to a close and it was time to head home. While all our gear was being packed up, we children scoured the river bank for some trace of the tiger. Sure enough, there we found enormous pugmarks running along the water's edge and up the embankment towards the area where the horses were kept. Wide-eyed, we looked at each other while Bruce said, horrified, "What if the tiger had eaten the horses? How would we get home?"

Back up the mountainside towards home, in single file, on the narrow mountain path we headed. First in line was Father, then Mother and us children, followed by the servants and lastly the coolies. Hearing the excited conversation between the servants and the coolies, in a tribal language I did not understand, curiosity got the better of me and I asked in Assamese, "Kijung, what are they talking about?"

"Oh Missy Baba, it is terrible. Only two days ago in that field behind our campsite, a big old tiger carried off a woman who was working in a field."

"Did he eat her?" I asked.

"I don't know, but she was screaming and kicking as he carried her deep into the jungle and the villagers never found her, only pieces of her clothing were found stuck to a tree," he shuddered. Without saying another word, I felt my bag full of rocks and quartz tied to my saddle and thought to myself that it's fun to go camping, but it's much safer at home where we at least had real, sturdy walls.

Philip Adams - the British D.C., an aide to the governor, Lady Reid, another aide, Mother, governor of Assam Reid, Audrey, Bruce, me, Jim and June, on a visit to us in Impur

Bruce and me watching a tribal dance performed for the governor of Assam

8
GHOSTS

Frank, an old family friend from America, had, for years, delighted in recounting a varied assortment of ghost stories. There was the one where his family would hear loud footsteps crossing the living room floor of his old Victorian house at exactly midnight at least twice a month. Then there was the one where, every night at exactly 2am, the windows of this same house would rattle and the bed would shake violently. That ghost was traced to a local freight train that crossed a nearby bridge, which in turn shook the ground in neighbouring areas.

As children growing up in the mountains of northeast India, we had several ghost encounters of our own. Mr Adams, the British District Commissioner for our district, was visiting us, along with his assorted aides and a complement of Gurkha soldiers.

One afternoon, while enjoying tea and cakes with my parents on our verandah, Adams looked out at the Menkong jungle, which covered the mountain that was directly across from our village. Between us and the Menkong was a deep valley. One mile down, at the bottom of this valley, was a swift river. On several occasions, my father would take us children with him, down the mountain to the river where he had constructed a small dam with which to generate enough power to charge the battery for his motorcycle. He was forever trying all sorts of methods to do this. One time, he ordered an enormous windmill from a mail order catalogue. This, also, was to be the 'ideal' method with which to charge the motorcycle battery. Unfortunately, Mother Nature did not cooperate, for there was never enough wind to turn the windmill. It sure looked like Minnesota though! It also provided an excellent lookout point for my brother and me.

Carefully setting his empty cup back on the saucer, Adams leaned forward and said to my father, “The Gurkhas tell me that there is a tiger living in the Menkong, who the villagers say shares the soul of an old man who lives in your village. They also say they know where this tiger is at this time”. My father smiled, a sly look coming over his face. “Tell you what,” Adams went on, “I’ll get my Gurkha sepoys to beat on the tiger, while you visit the old man and we will see if there’s any truth to the story”.

“I know who the man is”, said father, “but you must agree that your men will not kill the tiger. If there is any truth to their claim, I do not want the man’s soul on my hands.”

“Agreed,” exclaimed Adams. Synchronising watches, they agreed on a time for the next day when my father would visit the old man and the Gurkhas would beat on the tiger.

‘Beating on’ meant that they would first locate the tiger, then surround it and, slowly, with large machetes cut the jungle down, getting closer and closer, until they spotted the tiger and more or less had it contained. No one except Adams and my family knew of the plan. The Gurkhas were only told the following morning that they were to locate a tiger that had been killing some goats in the village. They waited until the hottest part of the day, when they knew the tiger would be sleeping.

At about 2pm the following day, my father took his walking stick and headed into the village to visit several of the families who lived there. All of us, including my mother, sat on the verandah, eyes glued to the distant dark green of the Menkong jungle. At approximately 2:30pm, we could see a ring of light green grow larger and larger, as the thick, dark jungle was cut away. We shivered with anticipation and wondered what was happening with the old man.

It was almost dark when Adams returned. Father had been back for several hours, but would tell us nothing. Following behind them as they walked together into the living room, we finally heard the outcome of their experiment. "I went into the old man's house", stated my father, "and we just talked about the village, his health and so on then at exactly 2:30pm, the time your men started to beat on the tiger, he became very nervous and agitated, to the point where, at the exact time your men closed in on the tiger, he ran frantically from the house. Poor old guy, he was terrified," laughed Father.

"Extraordinary", exclaimed Adams. "I've heard about this sort of thing, but never experienced it first hand".

"Afterwards, when I told some of the villagers about it," Father went on, "they said whenever there were tigers killing their cattle, the old man was always consulted, as they didn't want to kill his tiger, as then he too would die."

Several years passed and Adams was once again visiting us. In the course of the conversation, he asked about my father's work. When my father told him he was going to Bymo, a village on the border of headhunting country, Adams urged my father not to take the family along. "I won't tell you why, but I will write down my experience while staying there and put it in a sealed envelope. You do the same after you have stayed there and next time we meet, we'll exchange envelopes."

"Sounds great", smiled Father. He just loved these sorts of adventures.

The time came for Father to leave for Bymo. He was going to see if he could convince the villagers that they needed a small school.

Once again, all supplies were packed and loaded on the backs of the coolies. Dad and one servant travelled on his new motorcycle, even though the roads were not at all adequate. Many times, they would have to get off and push the heavy bike up a steep path or stop and cut back the jungle where it tried to reclaim the road. They arrived at the rest house or dak bungalow just before nightfall. Tamang, our servant who was with Dad on this trip, readied dinner and made up Father's bed. "I'm sorry, sahib, but the men and I will not be staying near the dak bungalow tonight; we will stay with some villagers," he said apologetically. "I will be here to make palang chai [tea]. Good night, sahib". With that, he turned and ran towards the thatched roofed houses in the village.

Retiring early, as he had endured a harrowing trip that day, Father was asleep in minutes. About 1:00am, he was awakened by a terrible odour. It smelled like decaying flesh. Sitting up in bed, he was startled to see a luminous green horse's head. "I must be dreaming," he said to himself. Getting to his feet, he walked over to where the head was suspended about four feet off the floor. When he put out his hand to touch it, it disappeared. The obnoxious odour took a while before it too disappeared. The following morning, Tamang was there early to see if my father had survived the night. "Now I know why you wouldn't sleep here," my father teased.

"Oh, sahib, the villagers say this bungalow is evil."

In returning to our home, my father had to pass through Mokokchung, where Mr Adams had his government headquarters. Adams was out in the territory, but his aide had an envelope for my father. Exchanging envelopes, my father tore his open and read, "At approximately 1:00am, an indescribable stench permeates the air, then an iridescent green horse's head appears. If you try to touch it, it disappears. Otherwise, it disappears after about thirty seconds. There is no logical explanation for this phenomenon as none of the locals own now, or have ever owned a horse".

Several years later, when Bruce was older, he and my father had occasion to return to Bymo. Once again, as soon as dinner was served and beds made, the help made a hasty exit to the village, leaving those crazy Americans to the evils, whatever they were, that lurked in the dark corners of that haunted dak bungalow. They were once again visited by the evil-smelling horse head.

My mother, two sisters and I never had the dubious pleasure of spending a night with the Bymo ghost. Actually, it so terrified my father that I was a mature woman before he would reveal to me what had happened to him in that lovely village.

Swedish Christmas in Nagaland

Several weeks before Christmas, we three girls were banned from Mother's sewing room. It was in here that she made clothes for us. Dresses, skirts, doll's clothes and pyjamas. Thank God, I would not have to wear Bruce's PJs for another year. How I hated the draught that chilled my tummy from that dumb opening in the front!

Cookies were baked and decorated. A small, thin pine

tree, which had been planted several years before, was cut down and cleared of bugs. It was placed in our living room and decorated with ornaments that were old but cherished. We children made paper decorations. These usually caught fire from the small candles on the tree. A nearby bucket of water was essential. Then Christmas Eve arrived and we had a delicious dinner of roast goose or chicken and even English plum pudding. After dinner, June, all dressed up in a green velvet dress, would play Christmas carols on her violin. Dad would read the story of Jesus' birth for the hundredth time and then all of a sudden, he had an extreme emergency to be tended to in his office across the lawn. Suddenly, we heard a gruff "Ho ho ho. Any good children living here?" Out of the darkness came this terrifying Santa Claus, dressed in a frayed, long, red coat and a peaked hood. On his back, he carried a big, red sack. The older children giggled, us younger ones shrunk back in terror, begging Mother to please call Father to come home. Standing by the Christmas tree, he gave out presents calling on us one by one. Many of the gifts had been purchased on the last trip to Calcutta. We had beautiful toys from England, among other homemade gifts. Every time that this scary-looking Santa turned to leave, he would bump the tree, as he couldn't see too well because his hood had slipped down over his eyes. Immediately, one or more of the candles would fall and start a fire. Luckily, we always got it out before too much damage occurred. Only when Bruce recognised the wedding ring on Dad's left hand did we realise why he was never there to see Santa.

9
IN THE SHADOW OF KANCHENJUNGA

June remembers that, at that time in colonial India, all foreigners who kept their children with them would send them to boarding schools in the mountains, to escape the torrid heat of the plains. At 6,000ft in the Himalayas, in beautiful Darjeeling, was Mount Hermon School - a British public school like Eton. The weather there was temperate and healthy all the year.

The students were of many different nationalities - English, Anglo-Indian, American, Scandinavian, Persian, Nepali and Tibetan. During World War II, many students came from Europe to escape the war.

The founder of the Mount Hermon School was an American Methodist missionary, Miss Emma Knowles, who was principal from 1895 to 1915 and called it Queen's Hill. Bishop Fisher established and changed the name to Mount Hermon in the 1920s. The curriculum was of the British public school Cambridge system and we had to take classes in eight to ten different subjects, from maths to science, Latin, French, Hindi, history, geography, English, physiology, scripture and domestic science.

All papers and tests of the Junior and Senior Cambridge were sent to Cambridge for marking and assessing. To this day, the school still exists.

Mount Kanchenjunga (over 28,000 feet), modern India's tallest mountain as seen from Darjeeling in the 1930s

Jim Recalls

Mother had done her best with home schooling and with three younger children still at home, it was time for June and me to go to boarding school in Darjeeling - a 700-mile trip to the top of the Himalayas. On the 1st March 1938, we went on the long five-day journey to Darjeeling to go to the Mount Hermon School. June, a precocious child of twelve, was Mother's pride and joy. I was but a lad of ten, eager to learn. We were enrolled at Mount Hermon, a co-ed school from 1938 through 1941.

The school term began in March and ran through to the middle of November.

After difficult farewells, we mounted our horses for the three-day trip to the railhead at Nakachari. June was on Raja and I was on Akokpa, followed by an entourage of coolies with our luggage, bedding and food. Proudest of them all, the Tiger Man, with a gun.

After camping at Khari and Lakhuni, we finally crossed the river at Chang Chang Pani and with the hills behind us, we entered the flat land of the plains of Assam.

Akokpa wanted to run and run he could, but for June's sake, who was too big for the ring saddle and was in danger of falling off, we dared not.

After a meal of chicken - the Naga TV dinner - we crawled under mosquito nets and tried to sleep, in spite of the jackals howling. There weren't any jackals in the Naga Hills, as there were too many eager spear chuckers. After a breakfast of shelled and fingerprinted hard boiled eggs, a bowl of 'Job's Tears' in KLIM from unhappy cows and tea, we were off. Dad said, "Job, overcome with grief, wept unashamedly and the tears striking the ground caused a hardy grain to sprout forth." We asked Mother if Job was really in the Naga Hills and she said, "Never mind. If Dad said it, it was true."

The bullock cart with our luggage creaked along a dusty road, past the native huts to the train station. On board and secured, we flew to the river at 30mph on the Assam Bengal RR. The Pandu ferry trip was a pleasure - a cool and quiet time to enjoy a delicious fish dinner on the gently rolling bosom of the mighty Brahmaputra, so far from its beginnings in the Himalayas, north of Kathmandu. I asked June how far it had come. She replied, "Thousands of miles."

By dark we were on the Bengal Mail in Parbatipur, enjoying the hawking vendors, cooking fires and enticing smell of native food. Morning at Siliguri and the narrow gauge Darjeeling and Himalayan toy train was waiting for the day-long pull of fifty-two miles to Ghoom, 7,000 feet above the plains. We started climbing slowly through a maze of switch-backs and reverse backs, where the train can back up into a spur. Sweating train men threw sand on the rails and piled on the coal, to take a run at the next high grade. When she couldn't make it, we backed down and tried again. We got off and took a steep footpath through the jungle to the next station, ate a banana and orange, threw rocks at the monkeys and waited for the train.

Kurseong, Tung, Sonada and Ghoom - the end of the rail line. The people look different. They are from Tibet, Sikkim, Bhutan and Nepal so have different dress and different languages. A lorry took us the few miles to Mount Hermon School, a substantial three-story masonry building in the shadow of Mount Kangchenjunga. You have to look above the clouds to see it. Chomolungma will have to wait until we get to Tiger Hill. Just then, the sun rose for a short time and her 29,000ft looked very small and far away. Tea Gardens and forests of pipal and cryptomeria covered the hills.

I felt this place needed a lot of exploring; won't be much time for school. Non scholae sed vitae discimus.

At one time, our parents rented the lower half of a cottage named 'Bide-a-wee'. There were many of these cottages in the area of the school where parents could stay while up there visiting.

June Recalls

Life in a boarding school was very strict and regimented and we lived by the bell. Out of the classroom, we were free to roam around the beautiful Mount Hermon estate. School uniforms were required and we wore navy blue wool jumpers, white blouses and long black stockings. The boys wore khaki or navy shorts and shirts and suits every Sunday.

The boys would collect beetles - the dung beetle and the stag beetle, six to eight inches long. One of the highlights of the school year was the annual ten-mile hike down the mountain to the Rangeet River. Before the monsoons arrived in 1941, we walked through the tea gardens below our school. The trip down was fun, sliding on the mud through the bushes and getting blisters, because no one owned Rockports or Reeboks in those days. We ate our bag lunch while dipping our sore and blistered feet in the river. Coming back up the mountain was another story, because we had used up our water and the heat was intense. We begged oranges off the Nepalis carrying them to market and decided to stop for a drink of water at one of the tea garden estates. The English tea planter invited our tired, hot bodies in for tea. What a delight - even a cake from Pliva's, the best restaurant in Darjeeling. Later, when we told the principal's wife about it, she said he'd been a recluse for ages, ever since his homesick wife left him and returned to England! He clearly enjoyed our company.

Jim Remembers

My favourite place was the girls' dormitory. It was on the third floor, protected by a phalanx of teachers at full alert on the second floor. Classrooms, library and dining room were on the first floor. The junior boys' dorm, Fern Hill, was a few blocks from school. Further down, the senior boys' dorm, River View - a long narrow building, originally a stable for a gentleman's horses. This had a metal roof. Strong arms and many stones pitched at the roof from Fern Hill woke them up, if all else failed.

There were a hundred and fifty students from twenty-five different countries. What experiences! We had long hours of class and study, field hockey, athletics, cricket, football, tennis and most importantly gilli-danda [the old, old Persian game is too involved to explain here]. During the monsoons, the playing field was under water, but we played on and in the water.

When the green parrots flew by the hundreds over the ridge by the tennis courts, some would always fly into the wire. We had a feast. We cleaned them and encased their fat bodies in clay. From a termite hill, we dug a chulha in the side of a terrace, lit a fire below and cooked well-done parrot. We then cracked off the burnt clay, sprinkled it with curry powder and devoured it. Dessert was sweetmeats and pastries being carried by boxwallahs on Tukyar Rasta [road] just below school. Never mind how, but with ingenuity and slight manoeuvring, the tasty food in their tin boxes could be ours, for free.

Mother would send homemade cookies to me and, no matter where I would hide them, the next time I looked they were gone. So, I put them in the trunk that brought our clothes from home and no more thievery, neither were there any bugs. Unfortunately, I could only eat one at a time as I had forgotten about the mothballs.

The rivalry and competition between our school and the four other boarding schools in Darjeeling was intense! Once a month, a social was held for the Junior and Senior Christian Endeavour groups in the Community House. Our innocent games were musical chairs, etc.

For diversion in the evenings, we would add to our collection of beetles as they swarmed around the street lights. It was a simple matter to knock them down with long bamboo poles. There were coal black rangits with three horns. If they bit you, they wouldn't release for five minutes. These powerful rangits had massive proboscises and two strong forelegs. If you struck a pencil behind its beak, in anger, he would place a foreleg over each end of the pencil and break it in half. The little green 'spadie' [Anglo-Indian term for beetle] was a strong flyer. If you took a spool of thread, placed a nail in the hole, tied the loose end to a hind leg, he would fly in circles until the spool was empty. Spools of thread were in short supply.

The flying parson beetle had black wing covers that looked like cut away tails. They had a nasty habit of flying around with a small stone in their claws to drop on other bugs for a warm meal.

Oh, yes, the dungies, always in pairs, one ahead and one behind, in beautiful choreography moving their precious load.

And the stags with symmetrical antlers mounted on black heads with brown wing covers. Beautiful. They would just fit in an empty box of kitchen matches. We each had one for racing at the dining room table. We lined up the dishes on the edges as barricades, then held the stags at one end and scratched their backs. In anger, they would scramble to the other end for a reward of bread and syrup. If a member of the staff came in the room, we got the stags in their boxes and on our laps under the table and quit laughing.

And the hathi, biggest of all - big enough in fact, for a steady hand to paint a Union Jack on its back and sell it to a Brit for an anna or two.

We needed money to buy treats at Muslim Hafiz - a little roadside shop. He would also take stamps; our folks wondered why we seldom wrote home. He also sold bidis (the little Indian cigarette), twenty-five in a pack, for less than a penny. Player's and English Ovals were a lot more. Smoking at school was forbidden. "We will have no devil's chimney among the students or staff". The first offence meant a verbal reprimand, the second offence resulted in a caning and the third offence mandated a trip home. So to be one of the gang, most of us smoked, but not on campus.

The cigarettes were hidden under 'black rock' in a tea garden near by. This huge boulder was also home to scorpions and poisonous snakes, which made it more exciting to sneak a smoke. We would always send the greenhorns in first and I don't remember anyone getting stung. After a couple bidis, it was time to chew sour grass to hide the smell. If we could still walk after the tobacco and coriander, it was back to school for supper, more compulsory study, back to the dorm and the sleep of innocence.

In true British tradition, Boy Scouts was a very important part of school life and there were unlimited mountains to climb, rivers to cross, miles of hiking trails in the jungle and lost people to find and save.

One of the upper class girls, a chubby little orphan, had a problem staying on campus and in fits of despair would run screaming through the jungle. On an earlier occasion, she was gone overnight and a search party finally found her collapsed in a state of shock at the gates to a Catholic cemetery. The next time she ran away, it was up to the Scouts to find her, so trooping our colors, loaded down with food, water and climbing equipment, we would dash into the jungle calling her name and glad to be out of school. The natives could usually tell us where to find her and we would triumphantly return in time for tea or supper. This was so much fun we had to do it more often. We pooled our stamps, picked up some sweets at Hafiz and gave them to her if she would run away again. She did, so along came the colours to succour the damsel in distress. It worked a few times, then one day she was no longer at school. Word was that her folks wanted her home, but we always thought that she was an orphan. Maybe the school wanted the Scouts back in class.

Once a year, the Scouts were allowed a one-week extended hike to Jorepokhri or Sukhiapokhri, about ten miles from Ghum. These were small reservoirs for storing water. The last time I went along, it rained for eight days and nights out of seven! We were wet to the skin and our food turned to mush edible by spoon only. Our Scout Master, a New Zealander, said the Maoris would call our food 'miss mash' or missionary, well-done. Playing in the jungle, one Scout found a leech stuck to the roof of his mouth. It took four Scouts to hold him down while two more dug out the bloodsucker with a Scout knife. Along the road, one boy tried to pet a large monkey and was rewarded with a severe bite on the wrist. In the rain, our crippled troop started for school, cold and hungry, singing, "Pack up your troubles in the old kit bag and smile, smile, smile".

Field day was a big event, as we would compete against students from other schools in Darjeeling. The one big event was chariot racing: pyramids of seven boys, four on the bottom, two standing on their backs and a driver on top of those two, standing on their shoulders, holding on to two Scout poles for balance.

We were supposed to run around the track and win, without falling down. Even though we were cheered on by our classmates, we always fell down. Forget cricket. Hockey was fun, but if the opposing team consisted of Indians, out of politeness and lack of skill on our part, we would let them win. Baseball was unheard of and gilli-danda was fascinating. Our wind was good, our legs strong, but try as we might, we could never catch the woodcutters' daughters, whom we loved to chase and who could run like the wind, even carrying a heavy knife and basket full of wood. We had to save our strength as we neared the village, for it was necessary to turn and run rapidly up the steep hill as soon as we could hear the village men cursing. I tried to discourage this game, but all in vain.

The magnificent Himalayas above Mount Hermon School in Darjeeling

June & Jim at Mount Hermon School in Darjeeling

Audrey Recalls

On the 5th May 1938, June had a terrible pain; it was appendicitis. She nearly died, as the anaesthesia was too much for her. They stopped surgery and she had to come home and recuperate, but went back for the surgery on the 26th May. Again, she had a long wait and did not come home until the 6th June. She was so thin and undernourished, so they gave her a bottle of some sort of drink to increase her appetite. Jim and I had to take a nip of this drink as it sure did smell good. Then in October, Dad came up to Darjeeling as he had gone back to Impur. June and Jim were then put into boarding at this school. The other five of us left to go home where Mother would continue our schooling.

June Recalls

One event clouded the spring of 1938, when I had appendicitis. Fortunately, it occurred when Mother and Dad had rented a cottage on the school campus, so I was not alone with the grumpy school nurse. Major Drummond of the British Army rode out on his beautiful horse, Charger, to the school to examine me and give Mother a diagnosis. SURGERY! I was taken to the Eden Sanatorium in Darjeeling - the tea planters' hospital - and prepared for surgery.

Shortly after, I was carried upstairs to the surgery room by the Indian orderly because there were no elevators. The nursing matron came to my hospital room and turned down the bed. I was brought down from surgery unconscious and very pale as I had suffered a very allergic reaction to the anaesthetic (paraldehyde), obviously an overdose for me, a twelve-year-old girl. Mother asked, "Is it over already?"

The nursing matron replied, "You should be glad she is alive." We returned to the school campus.

A month went by and the pains were recurrent. Again, the Major rode out on horseback to talk with us. He said, "I will give her the chloroform myself and remove the appendix." This time the surgery was successful.

While I was still hospitalised, the hearse passed by the window and the nurse quickly drew the drapes. I wondered why and was later told by Mother and Dad that a sweet little six-year-old Swedish girl had died of pneumonia. The family was in India as the father worked for the Swedish Match Company. In 1938, there were no antibiotics available to save a little one's life.

Ten days passed and I was eagerly discharged, sore but recuperating and glad to be alive.

On the 24th May 1941, an Empire Day concert was staged with songs and scenes from Britain and its Empire. An American boy, John Jay, was dressed as a Cook's travel agent. Girls in sleighs sang Jingle Bells. Some represented New Zealand in a Maori dance and a lifelike kangaroo stole the show in a visit to an Australian homestead. Lastly, Doris Hunt gave a rousing recitation of Gunga Din. The climax depicted Britain at war, with senior students resplendent in service uniforms, marching past Dulcimer Lacy as Britannia, singing, "There will always be an England" and "Rule Britannia". The proceeds from the concerts went to the Red Cross.

Another highlight in the school year was our annual trip to Tiger Hill in October. There we waited for sunrise over Mount Everest. We would awaken at about 2am and hike twelve miles in the inky darkness to Tiger Hill. This was our most exciting outing and not to be missed. It was here that the boys and girls could walk hand in hand under the eye of a benevolent teacher. Tiger Hill was at an elevation of 11,000ft and it was a magnificent sight to behold, as we were surrounded by the snowclad Himalayan Mountains, most of which were over 20,000ft high. The rising sun touched one after the other in radiant colours of rose, pink, gold and then dazzling white. Mount Everest was among them, far away. On the return trip, we hiked to Ghum train station and drank hot sweet tea out of earthen chattis, before boarding the toy train for the journey back to school. The Darjeeling Himalayan Railway was a small old train with engines made in Scotland at the turn of the century.

The monsoon season began in the middle of June and storms of great magnitude poured with wrath down the mountain. Many roads became impassable and landslides occurred all over the hillsides. Homes and families were washed away. In 1899, a Methodist missionary family lost all six of their children in a landslide that swept away their home. Later, a girls' school and hotel for visiting missionaries was built as a memorial. It was known as the Lee Memorial in Calcutta.

In 1940, there were several military cantonments in Darjeeling and in the nearby towns of Lebong and Jalapahar. One day, a young soldier's wife was out with her toddler when they were caught in a deluge. The force of the wind and the rain knocked the baby out of her arms and into a deep nullah, or drain, along the road. The child was washed away and the body never found.

Going home day was excitedly anticipated. We looked forward to going home after nine long months away from our loved ones. Banquets were held and my class, the pre-Seniors gave the Seniors a lovely dinner in the teachers' drawing room. I bought some pale aqua taffeta from a store in town and had the school 'dirzee' (tailor) create a dress from a picture I found in a magazine. My dear friend Helen, the only other American girl in my class, wore a stunning burgundy silk made by the same man.

Going home day songs were sung, even in our daily chapel services. Those of us from Assam left a day or two early and Dad was usually waiting for Jim and me at the Nakachari railroad station. The main group of homeward-bound children rode the historic Darjeeling Himalayan Railway, commonly know as the toy train because of its small size. The old train puffed and pulled the trainload fifty miles to Siliguri - a town on the plains. Most of the students purchased malacca canes, water pistols and little paper bombs. The poor Nepalese people who gathered at the little stops on the railroad took a real beating from the jubilant trainloads of students: apart from the drenching they received from the water pistols or the stink bombs exploding at their feet, they had to take cover from the swish of a malaccan cane.

The canes were helpful in keeping the monkeys out of the open windows on the big train from Siliguri to Calcutta.

Jim Remembers

It's well up into October now, very cold, no heat in the buildings and the wind right off the snow pack. It was time to leave for home. Going home songs were sung and sobering goodbyes said. Little did June and I realise, we would never again laugh and cry and walk those sacred halls as students. Pearl Harbor was soon to be and then the war. By March 1942, our family was on a navy ship bound for the US.

More goodbyes at the railroad station in Ghum as we boarded the toy train for the trip down to the plains. And then I saw the little handcars used by the track maintenance crew and remembered hearing about senior classmen who would rent the little cars, mount two red flags on board and coast down the fifty miles to Siliguri. On the flats, the native children would give a helping push and going through the Terai - the most jungly part of the trip - we would sing old school songs loudly, to keep the leopards away. As you approached the station, there was a long stretch of level track and if you were too tired to pump, you could smoke a bidi and wait. Old Pufferbelly, with a scream of its whistle, was along and pushed us into the station in style.

On the train, June argued with the coolies as they loaded our two trunks, two bed rolls for sleeping, a tiffin basket with food, dishes and nimbu pani [limeade], plus Trixie the dog. Dad wanted to improve the blood lines of the Naga dogs and had procured a black Alsatian puppy, a female from an imposing German lady at school.

The dog, cowered, whined and would not walk on a leash. I told June we should leave the dog. "No, she said, you can carry her." And carry her I did, from train to train and ferry to train. But, most embarrassingly to me, every time I picked her up, she would wet on me with no shame. When we finally got her home, Dad gave the worthless dog to the Semas for training. We found out years later, they stuffed her with warm bananas and overripe pineapple for a centrepiece at a big feast.

The trains in India had separate coaches for men and women and, being a child, I thought I should ride with June in a ladies' coach. But the native women took offence at my being there and insisted that I ride with the men. So, the station guard put me off and I waited on a bench for the train to start moving. As it picked up speed, I ran for the women's coach; the guard couldn't keep up as I jumped for the step. The women locked the door from the inside. Not to be outdone, I took a good hold on the brass handrails and with June yelling encouragement through a window, I rode twenty miles outside to the next station. The elephant grass and bamboo practically tore the clothes from my body and the hair from my head.

Nakachari again and the Naga men brought horses and food for the trip home. Mother had sent delicious homemade cookies, cake and bread. Wonderful. We had been away for nine long months and would be home in three short days.

The horses were eager to go as we approached the bridge over Chang Chang Pani and we were watching for fruit in the river, larger than grapefruit with the colour and skin of an apple. Dad called them Apfel-China, but they are not oranges. We reminisced about an earlier trip on the motorcycle with Dad in this same area, when we happened upon a group of men with elephants, hauling teak logs out of the jungle. We stopped to watch and were invited to ride the huge beasts as they pulled and pushed the heavy logs to the road and rolled them around into an orderly pile, using their feet, trunks and capped tusks. The tusk points were polled and fitted with heavy brass caps to prevent splitting as they work. They have five toes on the front feet for more power and four on the rear. You can always identify a work elephant as the thin outside edges of its ears are badly torn from the mahout pulling himself up to his perch.

What a thrilling ride it was as we clung dearly to heavy ropes on the back and the mahouts yelled encouragement as they drove their hooks into the elephant's head.

Once the logs started moving, the pusher at the back with a coconut fibre pad on its forehead would back off and away we went, shearing off saplings and sliding over boulders. The elephant was steered by the mahout kicking behind one ear or the other. After work, it was down to the river for a bath and a good scrubbing by the crew. "Had they been fully immersed in the water, they would be good Baptists," Dad said. In the very early days of travel in the Naga Hills, there were no roads and missionaries rode elephants in the rivers, safe from snakes and tigers.

Back to the horses and a few steep miles up to Lakhuni, which was our first stop.

The next day, after a good start, we were about to climb Khari Hill and while stopping to watch the hornbills in the big trees, one of the men pointed out the pugmarks of a tiger in the dust of the road. The path up Khari, on the always shady side of the hill, was too steep and slippery to ride. So, I grabbed the horse by its tail and hung on.

Out of Khari village early, escorted by dozens of yelling children with a risky habit of pulling hairs from the horse's tails. We stopped for lunch at the old relic of a swinging bridge over Melak Pani, built by a previous missionary who, in his second year of college, changed his major from structural engineering to philosophy. The weird assortment of rope, boards and wire probably was a thing of beauty once, but was now safe for pedestrians only, so the men took the horses down to ford the river. Uphill, then down, all the way to the mission station. As we neared the village, we were met by a happy, smiling welcome party carrying bananas and warm lemonade.

On a previous trip up this same road, our party was

delayed by a tigress with two cubs, crossing in front of our nervous and spooky horses.

Down the hill to Impur, the mission station and there at the end of the road surrounded by oaks, pines and flowers, was our dear bungalow, a haven of peace and quiet in the heart of the Naga Hills. Mother, Dad, Audrey, Bruce and Bea welcomed us with open arms. It took a long time to catch up on all that had happened while we were gone.

10
WAR IN ASIA

Though the people of Europe and the United States may have nervously watched Hitler's march through Europe in the late 1930s, in India, we children were blissfully unaware of world unrest. Our parents may have known that the Japanese were quietly amassing troops to lay claim to Asia and the south Pacific, but they invariably discussed private matters in Swedish, which we did not understand. Jim says our parents only told us three things: "Be good. Eat your food. Go to bed!" Even our parents may not have realised how grave the danger was: The Statesman, the only English newspaper available, took a week to be delivered from Calcutta. Even the mail took five days from Jorhat, as the dak wallah, or postman, travelled only by day, climbing trees at night for safety from wild animals.

My parents' second term in India would end in 1941 and they were negotiating for passage to the United States. Delayed though news was, that year the papers were full of reports of worldwide danger. The Japanese attacked Pearl Harbor in December 1941, causing great loss to the American Navy and bringing the United States into the World War. The Japanese were also positioning a large army on the border of Assam. Thousands of Indian refugees poured into the Naga Hills, increasing the fear that we might not be able to leave India for the duration of the war. My parents contacted the American consulate but they returned conflicting telegrams: one day telling them to move out and the next to remain in Impur, causing Mother to pack and unpack suitcases daily. One day my father had already ordered our suitcases down the hill when a message came telling us to wait; he had to send a runner to the porters to return to Impur with their loads.

At last, they decided to leave regardless, hoping a way would appear for escape. We found the railway station was absolute bedlam, as we encountered hundreds of refugees from Burma trying to outrun the Japanese.

War had become a cruel reality to these people, who recounted the brutality of the invading army. On the train to Calcutta, we followed blackout procedures and in the city we found carefully guarded and sandbagged government buildings, anti-aircraft artillery in the Maidan, or parade ground and sirens to signal air raids. The US consul in Calcutta directed us on to Bombay, where we boarded the Wakefield, a former luxury liner turned troop ship. The ship was being refitted in Bombay after being bombed in Singapore and my parents were grateful that we had at last found passage to the US, though later we learned that the Wakefield had transported 6,000 troops, mostly Canadians, from North America to Singapore. Many of the soldiers aboard the ship when she was attacked in Singapore harbour were taken prisoner. They were later forced by the Japanese to construct a bridge, now famous because of David Lean's movie, *The Bridge on the River Kwai*.

My father had to sign every one of us, including my seven-year-old self, into the US Navy. He paid thirty-five US dollars each for our travel, or the equivalent of a dollar a day.

My mother, us girls and Bruce were given an officer's cabin on the A deck, while Jim and Dad were billeted below in pipe berths on the D deck with the ship's crew. Among the other passengers were many wives and children of the American-owned Burma Oil Company, also escaping the war. The ship sailed first to Madagascar and then on to Cape Town, South Africa, where we stopped briefly and went ashore. Mother and Jim contracted hepatitis there.

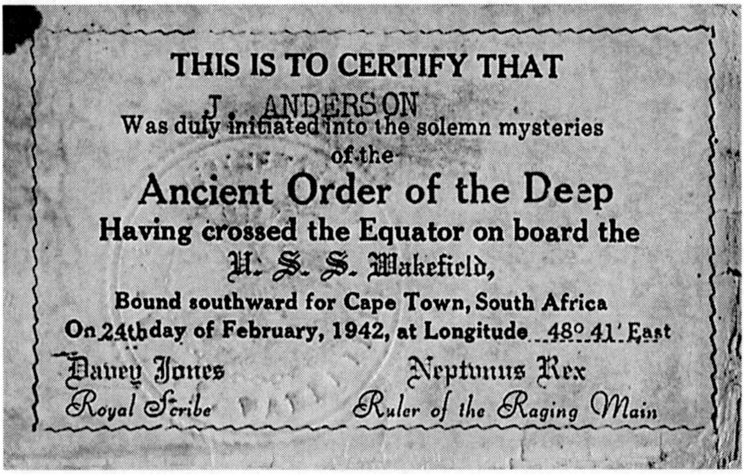
THIS IS TO CERTIFY THAT

J. ANDERSON

Was duly initiated into the solemn mysteries of the

Ancient Order of the Deep

Having crossed the Equator on board the

U. S. S. Wakefield,

Bound southward for Cape Town, South Africa

On 24th day of February, 1942, at Longitude 48° 41' East

Davey Jones — Royal Scribe

Neptunus Rex — Ruler of the Raging Main

June's initiation into "The Ancient Order of the Deep" on board the troop transporter "The Wakefield"

Jim has never forgotten getting deathly ill on the upper level of a double decker bus and throwing up on all of the people below. One of the Wakefield's sailors fared even worse. He was killed in a brawl in Cape Town and the authorities returned his body to the ship, where it was unfortunately stored in a galley freezer. The other sailors insisted that was why food aboard ship tasted so bad.

Bad food and all, in February and March of 1942, we sailed westward through the Atlantic and along the east coast of South America, hoping to avoid enemy submarines. At night, we endured total blackout; with our portholes closed and no air conditioning in the tropics, sleep did not come easily, though Jim and Dad were allowed to sleep on deck. The crew weighted the trash (but left the dead sailor in the freezer!) and only threw it overboard at night. Day and night, we sailed a zigzag course, changing the boat's heading every ten minutes, as German submarines required nine minutes to re-aim their torpedoes. Passengers and crew conducted lifeboat drills regularly.

Only two days out of New York, an American destroyer met the Wakefield to escort us into New York harbour. I vaguely remember the lifeboat alarm waking me at around eleven that night. Soon we heard depth charges explode - clearly a German submarine was in pursuit. A sailor kept Dad, Jim and the other male passengers on the D deck at pistol point and we all feared we might be separated forever. The destroyer stayed nearby and we must have gotten the better of the German Navy, as we never had to man the lifeboats. Later we learned that another troop ship headed for New York had been torpedoed and sunk not far behind us.

On the 21st March 1942, I watched from the ship's port side with the other passengers as we passed the Statue of Liberty. She looked grand enough as we sailed towards the Brooklyn Ship Yard. Still, though I had been born in the United States, I was not thrilled one bit to return. I considered myself Naga to the core. Later, while we were staying in a New York hotel, government officials approached my parents, hoping to recruit my older brothers and sisters to return to India as military translators. If only they had asked me! I would have returned to India, in a New York (not Indian!) minute.

Far away from our safety in New York, Singapore fell to the Japanese early in 1942 and, by April, Burma was also occupied. The Japanese used Burma as a staging ground, with a strong air force and landing strips, hoping to capture the Imphal plain in India and thus to control Assam, cutting off air traffic to China over the Himalayas. The bombing of Imphal began in May of 1942. The Japanese also asked more than 45,000 Indian and Malay soldiers to transfer their loyalties from the British Crown to Japan and nearly 20,000 Indian soldiers actually joined the Indian National Army (INA), believing the Japanese promise that they would drive out the British and deliver freedom to India. Their leader, Subhas Chandra Bose, later known as Netaji, was a leader of the Indian Congress Party. Though Netaji openly cooperated with Germany and Japan, Mohandas Gandhi was among his supporters - hardly a surprise when one considers the Indian nationalist goal was to separate from Britain and become an independent state. Netaji mysteriously disappeared around the end of World War II and the Indian independence movement mourned his loss.

Early in the war, Britain's Lord Mountbatten, later Viceroy of India, pleaded with President Roosevelt for help saving India for the Crown. The question was given priority attention at the Quebec Conference in 1943 and the US and Britain agreed not only to supply air transport to India but also dedicated experienced air crew and one hundred new C-47A planes in the first ever American commando force, which served in India.

By then, both the British and Japanese forces were formulating new strategies to attack the other side. The Japanese attacked Kohima, north of Imphal, on the 5th April 1944, with their 15,000 troops. The British military was ordered to cut off the Dimapur-Imphal road. This would stop the supply of ammunition, medicine, food and water from falling into the hands of the Japanese.

At the beginning of the battle, the small garrison of 3,500 British soldiers, without an airstrip, held all the hills which were in a commanding position above Kohima. These British troops were pushed back by the Japanese soldiers, who dug in on the higher ground. The fighting was so close that the district commissioner's garden was divided in the middle, by the Japanese and the British. This area later came to be known as 'no man's land'. They were not shooting at each other anymore, as they had no more ammunition, but hand to hand bayonet charges were exchanged. Over six hundred casualties were handled by Colonel Young DSO, a British doctor and his Indian staff.

While Kohima was being attacked, the Imphal valley was completely surrounded in all directions by the Japanese Army.

The propaganda from the British government to the local people was that the Japanese were invading Manipur and India. Therefore, the INA along with the Japanese Army did not receive as much help as they had expected from the natives.

During this time, two Japanese soldiers disguised themselves as local Naga workers. The British employed a large number of Nagas as labourers and housekeepers. These two Japanese soldiers in disguise stole an aircraft from the Palel airstrip. They used the aeroplane to drop leaflets stating that the Japanese and the INA were, in fact, friends of India and that they were trying to free India from Britain. They had to show the picture of Netaji with Mahatama Gandhi. By that time, Manipur already had a large number of followers of Gandhi's Indian National Congress and they knew about Subash Bose's earlier role in the Congress Party. Finally, several locals joined the INA and underground movements started.

The British Army immediately collected all the leaflets by offering large sums of money to those Indians who were loyal and brought the leaflets to them.

In the north, the 14th British Army was advancing to relieve Kohima. One Captain wrote in his diary: "I landed from a Dakota on an Imphal airstrip in early April 1944. There had been an air-raid warning while we were in flight from Comilla and we had to turn back to Silchar and wait. When we arrived, there was a blazing plane at the end of the runway and gunfire at the distance. I had been through the Blitz but this was real war and not like the movies. The Japanese 15th Division had surrounded the town and here in the north had dug in on a number of dominating peaks, including those sitting astride the only road north. This road led to Kohima (itself besieged by the Japanese 30th Division). The countryside was steep, partly jungle, with deeply cut ravines running down from the heights above. We had just gone across one of these with difficulty to the other side of the mountain, when the distinctive rattle of an enemy light machine gun opened up and everybody hit the ground."

On the 11th June 1944, the Cargo Combat Squadron sent aircraft to Imphal, on their first mission into combat. By that time, it was clear that the locals were sympathetic towards the Japanese, so any strategic discussions were to be held in the absence of the local people. The fighting in the valley resulted in several losses.

Tokyo Rose, the female voice of Japan's radio propaganda campaign, broadcast the news of all the casualties the next day and even listed the names of the dead crew members, as well as the identifying numbers of the aeroplanes.

The landing at Imphal airstrip was tricky, although Japanese aircraft were not much of a problem because they were fighting in Arakan. However, Japanese ground firing was continuous from the hilltops. By then, this strategy was no longer unknown to the Royal Air Force. RAF fighter aircraft would circle the valley several times in order to confuse the Japanese artillery, allowing the cargo planes to land quickly on the airstrip below.

This air campaign was successful. The siege of Imphal was as costly for the Japanese as Flanders was for the Germans in World War I, for here on the 'Bloody Plains', 50,000 of Japan's best soldiers lost their lives.

By early August 1944, monsoon season was at its peak. Heat, mosquitoes, and shortages of food and ammunition all caused a lack of enthusiasm and willpower among the Japanese soldiers to proceed further. They were hungry and sick with malaria.

These retreating Japanese soldiers were provided with help, food and shelter by local inhabitants of the hills and plains of Manipur.

The Japanese Army, for the first time, was fighting a retreating war, but not until many more lives were lost on both sides. After the conquest of the Imphal battle, Lord Mountbatten went to Sylhet and thanked the American Combat Cargo Groups personally.

World War II ended after the atomic bomb Little Boy was dropped from Enola Gay, the American B-29 bomber, at Hiroshima on the 6th August 1945 and another bomb was dropped at Nagasaki three days later. In a true sense, the rescue of Imphal-Kohima could be described as the

Normandy of the east. Later, World War II memorial cemeteries were established both at Imphal and Kohima. The Imphal cemetery has 1,300 British burials, 10 Canadians, 5 Australians, 220 Indian, 40 East Africans, 10 West Africans and 10 Burmese. A more or less equal number of soldiers from these forces are buried at Kohima.

The forgotten Imphal-Kohima War will come to life every time you visit these war cemeteries. The burial sites are marked with bronze plaques recording the anguish and sacrifice in the following inscription at Kohima: 'when you go home tell them of us and say for your tomorrow we gave our today'

But in the United States, the Anderson family was suffering other consequences of war's upheaval. Jim, Audrey and our mother had contracted hepatitis during our travels, presumably in South Africa where Jim first got sick and all three came down with jaundice in Buffalo, New York, where we had gone after leaving the city. The rest of us were taken in by various families among the churches our father was visiting as a missionary. I was lucky enough to stay with a kind family whose older daughter showered me with her old paper dolls and toys - a real treat since most of our playthings had been left behind to await our return to India. I do have the well-worn, amber-eyed teddy bear and small wicker chair that travelled with me on the Wakefield from India, which remained with me all my life. Teddy sits quietly in my office to this day, the first and dearest of the more than twenty bears of all shapes and sizes that I've collected in my travels.

After the invalids recovered, we moved on to Warren, PA, to stay with Dad's cousin, Henry Blick. The only climate I had known was the warm days and cool nights of my beloved Naga Hills. Though I had seen the indomitable white peaks of the Himalayas, I had never before touched or tasted snow. At Henry Blick's home, I went out into the wet, white yard and made a snowman, which was even more fascinating than the playthings that had amused me in Buffalo.

I was a girl who had grown up in the jungle, completely comfortable in the outdoors. Delighted to experiment with this cold new phenomenon, I went about building a small snowman, which I proudly carried inside to display and preserve forever. Imagine my dismay when the small sculpture melted and disappeared into a puddle! This strange new world, however interesting, was occasionally quite distressing.

Soon we boarded the train west to Minnesota. After a brief visit to Saint Paul, we headed to Alexandria, Minnesota, where some of my mother's family resided. We must have seemed backwards and odd to our Minnesota cousins, who treated us coldly from the start. Perhaps this was Scandinavian reserve, except that our parents had been raised the same way and the Swedish cousins I've met as an adult are warm and welcoming. But we were jungle-dwellers whose clothes were out of style and we spoke with that peculiar Anglo-Indian chi-chi accent peppered with odd Britishisms, like tiffin for lunch and napkins for the baby's bum; we used serviettes to wipe our mouths. It didn't help when Bruce defended our speech as "continental", to the young people from Alexandria, which may actually be Lake Wobegon. Though neither Bruce nor I had yet attended boarding school, the three older siblings had gone to Mount Hermon and all their grades were sent on to Cambridge in England. They discovered their education had outpaced our American cousins. Jim, in particular, found that when his American teachers asked a question, his hand went up first and he stood beside his desk to offer an answer he'd known for years in the formal British style. This, predictably, created giggling and mockery from his classmates, who knew nothing of the protocol of British education. Our father was called in for a conference. Since Jim, to this day, is an unrepentant rascal, Dad naturally wondered what trouble his son had created. Never mind. Jim was promoted two grades, where he was less certain of all the right answers, not that he'd ever admit it.

My first recollections of any grandparent are in Alexandria. My mother's father was so kind. He had a cottage by a lake outside of town, where he took us all fishing. I had great fun on these expeditions, though Grandpa Lars spoke no English. Communication was nonverbal - good enough for a child who'd heard different languages all her life.

June finished high school in Alexandria, where she was valedictorian after only one year in school there. She was quicker to adapt than the rest of us and because of her stunning red hair and sweet personality, she was accepted by everyone, particularly any young men who came within twenty miles of her.

We moved to Saint Paul, where June entered nurse's training in the Cadet Corps, sponsored by the US government and Jim entered college at the University of Minnesota. Dad searched for a house in the city, but housing was difficult to find for a family with five children who wanted to rent for only a year. He sought help from Mr Nielsen, a Danish friend to whom my father had loaned money for food during the Depression. By this time, Mr Nielsen was a successful businessman and he not only found a home for us to rent, he also put up a large security deposit, lest the rambunctious Anderson children should wreck the place. We saw ourselves only as fun-loving, but we must have had a reputation as uncivilised. I have never completely understood this, though to this day I prefer not to wear shoes. My parents were always grateful for Mr Nielsen's help. However kind, he was a hard-living, hard-drinking man and it is a tribute to both of them that he and my father, a strict Baptist, were lifelong friends.

We spent two years in Saint Paul because the State Department refused to let my family travel until I was nine years old, an imposition I chafed under and have yet to understand. The difference in maturity between the ages of seven and nine still seems academic to me. I understood nothing of the dangers of the war or travel; all Bruce and I wanted was to go home, though by this time June, Jim and Audrey had adapted well to the States. Audrey had become popular at her high school and, like June, had a long string of boyfriends. Our parents must have seemed relaxed and trusting of their children for the time, but they were well aware of our unusual circumstances. We were all rugged and independent and the older children had been sent to boarding schools early, where they not only dealt with separation from the family, but also learned to manage the small allowance they were given for essentials at school. Audrey would show even more strength and independence than we expected when my parents were suddenly given notice late in 1944 that we must head for the East Coast and prepare for passage to India. At fifteen, Audrey still needed three years of high school to graduate and Mother and Dad worried about her coming back to India with us and then having to return to the United States on her own later. They quickly arranged a place for her to stay in the home of a Baptist church deacon our father knew, though Audrey had never met them. Though Audrey seemed to take it all in stride, she remembers taking her baby book, with its pictures and memories of the family and tearing it to pieces - an act she quickly regretted. She lived with the family in Saint Paul until she graduated, but she never felt like she really belonged there and the father insisted that she move out as soon as she finished high school.

She found a job at a bank and moved in with a friend from church until she could find an apartment. Audrey rarely talks about her feelings during this time in her life, but she admits to mixed emotions when pressed to discuss it. She had a strong group of friends from church, but she desperately wanted to return to India and she felt unloved because she was left behind. She understood that Bruce and I, so much younger, had to go back, but she admits the experience changed her forever.

She, June and Jim got together as often as they could, but only a few times a year. For a young girl on her own for the first time, the experience must have been devastating.

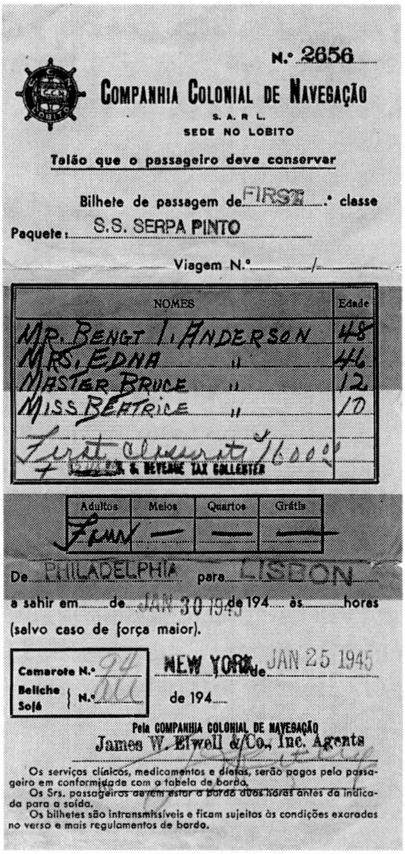

N.º 2656

COMPANHIA COLONIAL DE NAVEGAÇÃO

S. A. R. L.

SEDE NO LOBITO

Talão que o passageiro deve conservar

Bilhete de passagem de FIRST .ª classe

Paquete: S.S. SERPA PINTO

Viagem N.º /

NOMES		Edade
MR. BENGT I. ANDERSON		48
MRS. EDNA	"	46
MASTER BRUCE	"	12
MISS BEATRICE	"	10

Adultos	Meios	Quartos	Grátis
Four	—	—	—

De PHILADELPHIA para LISBON

a sahir em ... de JAN 30 1945 de 194... às ... horas

(salvo caso de força maior).

Camarote N.º 94

Beliche / Sofá N.º all

NEW YORK de JAN 25 1945

de 194...

Pela COMPANHIA COLONIAL DE NAVEGAÇÃO

James W. Elwell & Co., Inc. Agents

Os serviços clínicos, medicamentos e dietas, serão pagos pelo passageiro em conformidade com a tabela de bordo.

Os Srs. passageiros devem estar a bordo duas horas antes da indicada para a saída.

Os bilhetes são intransmissíveis e ficam sujeitos às condições exaradas no verso e mais regulamentos de bordo.

Our outgoing ticket on the Portuguese ship, "Serpa Pinto" sailing from Philadelphia to Lisbon, 1945

Back to India - 1945

We sailed from Philadelphia aboard the Portuguese ship the Serpa Pinto. She was a filthy, old bucket but quite safe, as the war was still on and Portugal was neutral. She sailed with lights blazing and dance music blaring right across the

North Atlantic, stopping briefly in the Azores, then on to Lisbon. We had a marvellous time in Lisbon with side trips to Sintra and all the gorgeous old castles. It was quite unnerving for us, as there were German officers and soldiers everywhere.

There was no immediate passage on towards India, so we were stuck in Portugal for the duration. We lived in a boarding house with several other displaced families. After approximately a month, we got passage on a Portuguese registered freighter.

From Lisbon, we sailed to the island of Madeira, where we did not go ashore. Vendors' boats came out to our ship and sold the most beautiful embroidered linens etc.

From Madeira, we sailed to the Canary Islands; I don't remember if we stopped there or not. Then on to Luanda, Lobito and up the Congo River, gorgeous and muddy like a giant brown serpent. We left our ship in Lourenço Marques - a jewel of a city on the Indian Ocean.

While there and waiting for a ship heading east, we stayed at the Polana Hotel, right on the beach. For a couple of kids, ten and twelve years old, it was heaven on Earth. There were just a very few guests there, due to the war. By this time, Bruce and I were conversing quite well in Portuguese. After many weeks and no hope of a ship heading to India, we took a train to Durban, where once again we stayed in a boarding house or mission home.

Later, while staying at this mission home we all got fat (and indigestion) on the rich milk and alligator pears (avocados). We made many side trips while waiting for a ship. My poor father was trying to hold classes for Bruce and me, as we were falling behind on our schoolwork. While in Durban, we received the sad news of President

Roosevelt's death.

Finally, after five months of being in transit, my father got us passage on an old minesweeper headed for India via the Seychelles. Once again, we were required to have total blackout and our evening walks on deck were beautiful but a little scary!

We sailed to the Seychelles - an absolute paradise! The tropical foliage was magnificent; it was like one would have imagined the Garden of Eden, but without the snake. We were there only a few days, then it was on to Bombay.

At long last we set foot on Indian soil. What a thrill to be 'home' again, in spite of all the changes. It was quite a shock to see British and American military vehicles everywhere. Their tanks lined the streets of Calcutta. Military personnel were running the railroads. Mixed in with the Indians were all the gum chewing, joke cracking American GIs.

After a brief stay to purchase supplies in Calcutta, we headed once again for Assam. Our first trip to the Naga Hills was to Kohima. What a shock: the entire town was demolished. One could barely see any buildings remaining from the fierce battle between the Japanese and British. Only one mission bungalow remained and it was greatly damaged.

Upon returning to Impur, I saw one little Naga wearing Japanese Army boots! I wanted to know where he got them. He smiled and slanted his eyes like a Japanese person and put out his hand to show me the Jap's height. He said, "The Japanese soldier was this high". You have to hand it to the Japanese who brought an army of men and materials over these mountains where there were no roads to invade Assam. There are all kinds of stories going the rounds of how the Nagas hindered their efforts. One patrol of about twenty-four Japanese soliders arrived at a headhunting village. The chief had butchered a pig and roasted it for the Japanese, seating them in a large circle with a Naga warrior behind each one. After a large amount of rice beer was served to the soldiers and the pork was consumed, the chief gave a signal and off came the heads of the Japanese. These heads were brought to the British District Commissioner, Philip Adams. He rewarded the Naga warriors a hundred rupees for each head.

Jorhat - 1945

When we arrived in Jorhat by train from Calcutta, we were shocked to find an enormous American air base where planes took off to fly 'The Hump' into China and Burma. There were signs of the war everywhere.

The GIs were so friendly to us and gave us everything and anything. Dad was given a Jeep, though I kind of think that he had his eye on a helicopter or two. Mother was happy to have all the tasty canned goods, bacon, cheese, vegetables, sauerkraut etc. Unfortunately, it was in gallon tins, which were too much for the four of us to consume in one or two meals. We had no refrigeration, so we soon had our Naga friends introduced to good old American grub. We surely didn't go hungry! I know Mother really appreciated the medical supplies that they gave her. We had enough sports equipment to furnish a whole school. Once we were settled in Impur, it was time for Bruce to go to boarding school at Woodstock in Mussoorie, which was 1,400 miles from Impur. Poor Mother had to pack supplies for him for nine months. I can remember sewing on his name labels for hours on end.

11
WOODSTOCK IN THE FOOTHILLS OF THE HIMALAYAS

The following year, I was sent to school with Bruce. Taking the train from Moriani, we headed for Calcutta, along with all our supplies for the nine months we would be away at school. This being my first trip away from home without our parents and being unaccustomed to dealing with such matters, I was afraid.

After crossing the territory then known as East Pakistan, guards pulled us from the train and thoroughly searched our entire luggage. Soon we were back on the train. There were hundreds of refugees; some tied themselves to the train, while others climbed on to the roof. The roof of the train was a solid mass of humanity. It was total chaos as the Hindus were trying to escape from the massacre by the Muslim Pakistanis.

Finally, the train was back in Indian territory. At each and every railroad station, we would hear bloodcurdling screams as some poor soul, whether Hindu or Muslim, would be beaten to death. We should have been relieved to be in Calcutta, but the situation there was worse. Hand grenades were being thrown at any suspected Hindu or Muslim.

At one point, the train stopped for several hours. When Bruce and I went to investigate, we saw a large crowd of people standing up by the engine. Pushing our way through the crowd, we could see that the engine had hit and killed a cow. No one would touch the cow, thus admitting that they were Muslim, as the train at that time was still in India. There was nothing else to do except for Bruce and me to drag the poor beast off the tracks so that the train could continue on its way. When we arrived in Calcutta, we were shocked to see that what once had been a beautiful city was now in ruins. Howrah train station was teeming with refugees from East Pakistan. Buildings were burned out, people were living like stalked animals in the streets and explosions rocked the city. It was terrifying.

My sweet Naga dog Keto

In Calcutta, we were joined by more students on their way to Mussoorie. Pretty soon, the student group grew as we picked up more kids at Lucknow and several other towns along the way. What a noisy raucous group we were! We hardly ever used the doors of the compartment, mainly climbing in and out of the windows.

When we were fed at the various train stations, it was the usual extremely hot curries, which were served on brass trays. It was always a quick lunch or dinner, due to the fact that once the local monkeys spotted the food, it was a race to see who could get it first - them or us. Most of the time it was the monkeys who ended up well-fed as they had the nasty habit of biting us. Once the train reached Dehradun, we were transferred to rickety old buses, which took us on the terrifying ride up to the Woodstock School. Many a bus had not made the treacherous trip and gone crashing down the mountainside. There were thirteen boarding schools in Mussoorie. We competed in sports with these other schools. Most of the students were missionary kids or children of foreign business people. There were also a number of Indians attending.

The friendships developed there have lasted to this day. One of my dearest friends, whom I've known since we were twelve years old, is Mary Chako. We still get together several times a year.

My Life At Woodstock

As with any group of teenagers, romances flourished - many of them lasting through long separations, eventually culminating in marriage.

The school was kindergarten through high school. I always felt so sorry for the little kids who seemed so homesick. We were very lucky to have been taught at home up to this point. The education we received from our parents was superb. When I returned to the US and entered a private school for my final two years of high school, I was repeating a lot of what Mother had taught me at ages nine and ten. In 1948, one of the boys at Woodstock came down with polio, so the entire school was quarantined for three weeks. Unfortunately, the young fellow died.

The school, which was founded in 1854, is built on the side of a mountain. Rhododendron trees covered with huge blossoms and towering pine and deodar trees grow in profusion. Boisterous langur monkeys leap from the treetops on to the tin roofs of the school buildings, making a huge racket. The aroma of the forest is intoxicating.

My daughter Roberta, a classical pianist, taught music at this school for one year and truly fell in love with the beauty of the area. From there, she moved to New Delhi where she taught piano and played many a concert. She has moved back to the States but still considers India home.

The political scene up at Mussoorie was a great deal less intense. The main problem for the students was the lack of meat. Occasionally, we were served dehydrated mutton and Bruce, along with some friends, shot a few langur. Of course, none of the school cooks would have anything to do with cooking them, but a few student mothers obliged and we ate monkey. The boys came through for many of us, as they often shot a deer with their homemade guns. Some of the mothers cooked it for us, as none of the Hindu servants would have anything to do with that either.

Dad's WWII jeep with lumber for the bungalow at Aizuto

Me with Keto and my brother Bruce

Dad's pride and joy

The Aizuto bungalow in recent times

Our lives at Woodstock gave us the opportunity to make many long-lasting friends. However, there were many times that we longed to be back in the Naga Hills with our friends there.

When Bruce and I were returning from our school year at Woodstock (I was thirteen, he was fifteen) we were driven by a man in an old rattletrap of a truck from the Nakachari train station as far as the road would permit. The driver dropped us off by a river where our servants were to meet us with our horses. We waited for hours and before long, it started to get dark. Darkness comes very quickly in the dense jungle. Terrified, Bruce and I climbed up a tree to wait. Not too bright a move, since leopards not only come to the river to drink but they also like to climb trees. At last we heard the nickering of the horses and the hushed conversation of the servants as they rounded the bend in the road. Thank God they brought Mother's homemade sandwiches, lemonade and cookies as we hadn't eaten before breakfast.

On another occasion, several miles from this river, at Chang Chang Pani, Kijung was to meet my father who was coming from a nearby village on his horse. Kijung often carried Dad's big rifle when he travelled alone in the jungle. While waiting for Dad to arrive, he heard the nervous coughing of Dad's horse but he could not see them. Soon he saw movement in the tall grass across the road. He then heard the familiar low growl of a tiger. His first thought was to shoot it; however, he only had one bullet. Terrified of missing but having no other option, he took a chance and shot. Luckily, the bullet hit its mark as the tiger roared, reared up and disappeared into the jungle. Dad,

Kijung and Raja (our horse) were safe. Several days later, workers in a nearby field found the body of the tiger.

12
AIZUTO - 1948

When we returned to Impur at the end of the school year, we were thrilled that we could be a part of building a new mission station in Aizuto. We now had an old US Army Jeep which would make the move to Aizuto slightly easier. We were extremely excited when we arrived in Aizuto and saw how beautiful the location was that our parents had picked out.

In 1948, the Indian Government had given us permission to build a mission station in Sema country. My father scouted the area and decided on a lovely location where there were natural springs. The Semas named it Aizuto, which means 'clear water' in the Sema language. Here Dad built a school, a small chapel and also a small temporary bungalow for us.

While he was holding a dedication of the mission by one of the ponds, the Semas who were with him swear that several evil spirits jumped out of the pond and ran up the side of the mountain in fear.

In Aizuto, the cook house was the first building that was constructed. It was where we lived while the bungalow was being built. Dad picked out the trees in the jungle that would be the best for the type of construction he had chosen. Stones were dug from the earth for the foundation and workers were brought in from Impur. We all pitched in to cut trees and clear the land.

Mother planted fruit trees and small pine trees were brought from Impur where she had started the seedlings. Methans - large wild buffaloes - were a constant threat, so the compound had to be fenced. What an exciting time that was! We thoroughly enjoyed our new home with the Semas.

A favorite pastime of mine was to hunt for quartz in the streams that ran through the mission compound. Christmas was always a memorable time, as we had a fantastic Christmas dinner with everyone that worked at the mission school and at the church. To this day I have many friends in Aizuto.

After graduating from Woodstock, Bruce was free to enjoy India for several months, as our ship wasn't sailing for some time. He travelled all across the country, joining a group of sadhus or holy men on a pilgrimage to Benares, swimming in the Ganges and hunting with the famous Jim Corbett. India was our home and all of us missionary kids love it dearly. The changes have been many, but we feel very fortunate to have been there virtually from the beginning.

On one occasion, my father was going to visit a village close to the headhunting border, so Bruce went along. With a fondness for living dangerously, Bruce convinced my father that he should travel across the border with one of Dad's Sema friends as an interpreter.

They hiked for several miles across the border to this village. At once, he was surrounded by crowds of naked children and even the dogs were curious. The children pulled at his red hair and pinched his skin trying to remove the strange white color. Many of the older people dropped to the ground in fear, thinking he was some kind of spirit.

Glancing up, he saw a naked old man approaching him. Behind him was his house, the front of which was covered with approximately one-hundred-and-fifty human skulls. This old man was the chief of the village. After checking out Bruce's strange hair and features, he invited him into his dark, smoke-filled house.

Through the interpreter, he asked many questions about Bruce and soon learned that he was not an apparition, but really a human being. The chief, bleary-eyed, dirty and naked, was truly impressed with Bruce. Raising his arm and yelling out some commands to several of the men gathered around him, they scurried out of the house and soon returned with a terrified young woman, wearing a small cloth skirt, her body dirty and covered with tattoos. Through the interpreter he said, "This is my eldest daughter; I give her to you as you must be a good spirit."

Being the diplomat that he was, Bruce told the interpreter to tell the chief, "I'm honoured by such a generous gift. However, I cannot accept your lovely daughter without a dowry. I must return home, but I shall return with several head of cattle." Smiling and showing a mouth full of black stubs that once were teeth (this from their habit of chewing opium), the chief agreed. Once Bruce and his friend were back across the border, they beat a hasty retreat home.

Kijung Ao with Naga warrior. The string of beads on this man's chest are brass skulls showing the number of heads he has taken

13
THE STATE OF NAGALAND

Growing up in Nagaland, we were unaware of the fact that there was a generous yearning on the part of the Nagas for independence. During and after World War II, it seemed to become more apparent. Then, after India became independent from Britain, the Nagas thought that they would be a separate nation as the British had indicated to them. This seemed to be inevitable. As late as the 1930s, when British rule was almost over, large parts of today's Nagaland did not even exist on their maps. Instead of showing villages, the maps showed large blank white spaces with the words "Unadministered and Unsurveyed".

But in 1947, India broke free of colonial rule. At the same time, rebels in the Naga territories sought their own independence from India. Many believed that they would create their own state of Nagaland in the most Baptist corner of the world, part of the most Hindu nation on earth. In Nagaland, nearly ninety percent of the people identify themselves as Christian. They formed the Naga National Council and adopted a slogan - "Nagaland for Christ". During the last fifty years, Nagaland has been ripped apart by a guerrilla war fought to establish a free Christian nation. Both Christianity and guerrilla warfare took root in the 1950s.

World War II brought chaos; independence and the separation of India and Pakistan brought slaughter and mistrust. I have seen the Naga rebels use Christianity as the present day reason to attack opposing elements, whether they are Nagas or Indian nationals.

The vast majority of Nagas initially supported the

freedom struggle, led first by the Naga National Council, which later became the National Socialist Council of Nagaland. The Naga nationalism gained momentum and was accelerated with the election of A.Z. Phizo as president of the NNC on the 11th December 1950. India tried to suppress them, sending troops in 1952. Three years later, the government banned missionaries from the region, believing they were stirring up the trouble.

But Christianity didn't fade. It exploded. Most scholars agree that the whole Naga problem was ineptly handled by the then police and administration. The banning of the NNC in 1952 compelled the leaders to turn underground once and for all. The ban was a blunder, because Delhi did not realise the popular support the NNC had at that time.

Before an attack or a hazardous march, Naga officers and men kneel to ask God's protection. In the camp mess rooms, no one dips his hand into his bowl before the most senior man present has said grace. Before he wraps himself in his blanket to sleep, a Naga soldier kneels to pray in silence. Most Nagas are Baptists. They were converted originally by American missionaries, who set up mission stations and schools in the Naga Hills and were finally expelled by the government of India soon after independence. Now, far from dying out, Christianity in Nagaland seems to be flourishing. The pastors are usually among the better-educated of the villagers and many of them speak English. Others are more or less permanently on the move, visiting a wide circuit of villages which have no resident pastor, distributing Bibles in the Naga dialects.

The Naga's spirit of independence and their readiness to fight for it, is far older than their recently-acquired Christianity.

A sixteen-point agreement was signed in 1960 and the State of Nagaland was born on the 1st December 1963. An analysis implies that the sixteen-point agreement was a mistake, as the demand of the people was for complete independence from India. This agreement is a remarkable document and it was the first of its kind signed by the government of India with any section of its people.

The generations of today cannot imagine the distress that the leaders of those days went through to take these choices. Many of these leaders were killed just because they voiced their feelings and convictions. They were true to the spirit of the Naga ancestors.

More recently, these 'Christian' Nagas are killing each other over the divisions of the various Baptist groups. Understandably, there was fear of the headhunters and the Japanese. However, to claim lives in the name of all that my parents and many before them had worked so diligently for, is heartbreaking. In retrospect perhaps, one realises that most wars are based on religion.

Many years later, my daughter Roberta, my sister Audrey and her husband Roger and I went back to all of these homes where we had grown up. What a thrill to visit with all of our playmates, walk through the villages and hear our Naga friends calling our names and hugging us, with tears in their eyes. We were welcomed into their homes and met all of their families. The biggest thrill was to once again be in the comforting arms of my ayah, who was now 89 years old.

Back to the USA - 1950

This term in India lasted only five years. Once again, we were eager to return to family and friends. We sailed out of

Bombay on the P&O liner, the Canton. Travelling with us were two girls from our boarding school who had graduated and were going to the US for college.

Our first stop was Aden, then Cairo, then Port Said. We had a great time sightseeing but when the ship was ready to once again sail, there was no sign of Bruce. The floating gangway had been removed and the engines were running.

All at once, there came a small boat racing towards our ship. Three people were waving frantically. They were my brother, his friend and the skipper of the boat. Rope ladders were lowered and, laughing, they climbed onboard.

From Port Said, we sailed through the Mediterranean and on to Southampton. After a brief stay in London, we sailed to Sweden on the Saga. While there, we met many relatives, including my father's father. We then sailed on the Stockholm to New York and finally had a marvellous reunion with my sisters and brother.

Dad's Arrest - 1954

In 1951, my parents returned to Nagaland. They were once again stationed in Kohima, which had been rebuilt after World War II. While there, they were to maintain the schools and churches. It was at this time that the Nagas were once again eager for independence from India. They often demonstrated, marching with banners and proclaiming, "We will fight for independence, just like the Americans did". This action, of course, put the burden of guilt on my parents, who were the only Americans living in Nagaland at the time.

These actions eventually got the attention of the Indian government people in New Delhi. Nehru, the Prime Minister, made a trip to Kohima to try and reason with the

Naga people. Fifteen thousand Nagas had gathered on the football field to hear what proposal the Indian government had for them. Standing at the podium, the Prime Minister declared, "When you Nagas get rid of the foreigners in your midst, we shall sit down and peacefully discuss your situation." He also did not address or even acknowledge the Nagas' request for independence from India. One by one the Naga delegation rose to their feet and walked off the field.

Shortly after this, several Indian armed soldiers appeared at my parents' bungalow, demanding to be let in to search the property. First, they seized an old shotgun, then some copper wire which they found in the attic and even some carbon paper from his typewriter.

My father was arrested and charged with having an "arsenal" in his home, having copper wire to communicate with China and treason against the Indian government. He was to be available for summons and under house arrest for ten months.

The American Baptist mission board hired a Muslim lawyer who fortunately got a not guilty verdict, but only after twenty-two court appearances. It was shortly after this that Bruce was diagnosed with terminal Hodgkin's disease, so my parents had to leave India hoping to see him before he passed away. Fortunately, the Indian government allowed them to leave the country. However, their visas were never renewed and their time in India was over.

Until his passing away at age 86, my father kept in touch with all of his beloved Naga friends. The Semas have opened the Anderson Theological Seminary in Aizuto and all of the Naga tribes have only fond memories of our family.

On the 14th August 1947, the Naga National Council claimed the right to independence. They boldly drafted telegrams to the press declaring independence for the Naga Hills. Twelve copies were addressed to the major newspapers. However, the postmaster sent them to the local District Commissioner, who was British. He decided that this declaration could only cause trouble, so he ordered them withheld. Therefore, no one in the government ever received them. The following day, India was granted her independence.

To this day, the Nagas still yearn for independence from India. However, the many factions and underground groups ignore the ceasefire agreements and still use violence against India, only to have Indian soldiers retaliate by burning down villages. Killing of many innocent people is done by both sides.

When I visited Nagaland in 1997, the bungalow that we built in Aizuto with so much effort had been converted into a hospital. Many of the nurses that were trained by my mother and the Mission Hospital in Jorhat are still working there. The Anderson Theological Seminary is run by the local Semas and is doing quite well.

How very thankful we Andersons are that we were raised in such diverse surroundings and with parents who took each situation that they were faced with and dealt with it with care, love and often a great sense of humour. We learned resilience, tolerance, compassion and, with me, an undying love of nature and animals. No situation we faced, whether it was illness, violence or even Dad's many arrests made us angry or bitter. We learned at a very early age to roll with the punches. As children, if we were bored we would make up games. If Mother was lonesome when Dad was away, we would cheer her up by being quite naughty. Life was never boring; it was great.

About the Author

Bea Anderson Swedien's parents Bengt and Edna Anderson lived in India from 1926 to 1955, returning to the United States every seven years on furlough. While on furlough in 1934, Beatrice was born. She was the youngest of five siblings. The Anderson family returned to India in the spring of 1935.

In 1942, on the family's next furlough, passage was secured on an American troopship, the USS Wakefield. Two days out of New York the ship was under attack by a German submarine. Terrifying though this was, the ship made it safely into Brooklyn Navy Yard.

A year later, due to the war, the return trip to India took five months. Living in the remote jungles of Nagaland which is on the border of Burma, she was home schooled until she was twelve years old, at which time she was sent to boarding school in Mussoorie, which is located in the foothills of the Himalayas.

In 1950, Bea returned to the US. In 1953, she married Bruce Swedien, a successful music-recording engineer, producer, composer and author. They now live in Ocala, Florida.

INDEX

Also from MX Publishing

Ssh! Lose Weight in 20 Minutes

By introducing small and realistic goals that fit into even the busiest schedules, weight loss is quickly and easily achieved. Importantly, it is sustainable because no radical lifestyle changes are required. So obvious and so simple - it works!

Play Magic Golf

How to use self-hypnosis, meditation, Zen, universal laws, quantum energy, and the latest psychological and NLP techniques to be a better golfer

Recover Your Energy

NLP for Chronic Fatigue, ME and tiredness

More books at www.mxpublishing.co.uk

Also from MX Publishing

Seeing Spells Achieving

The UK's leading NLP book for learning difficulties, including dyslexia

Psychobabble

A straight forward, plain English guide to the benefits of NLP

You Too Can Do Health

Improve your health and wellbeing, through the inspiration of one person's journey of self-development and self-awareness using NLP, energy and the secret law of attraction

More books at www.mxpublishing.co.uk

Also from MX Publishing

Process and Prosper

Inspiring and motivational book from necrotising fasciitis survivor Wendy Harrington. Amazing book for anyone facing critical trauma.

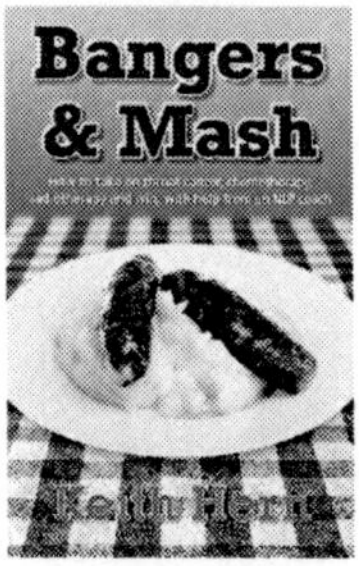

Bangers and Mash

Battling throat cancer with the help of an NLP coach. Keith's story has led to changes in procedure in many cancer hospitals and is an inspiration to cancer patients everywhere.

Performance Strategies for Musicians

Tackle stage fright and performance anxiety using NLP.

More books at www.mxpublishing.co.uk

Lightning Source UK Ltd.
Milton Keynes UK
UKOW011032071011

179923UK00001B/7/P

9 781780 920030